BRITAIN AT WAR
WOMEN'S WAR

Martin Parsons

WAYLAND

Editor: Jason Hook
Designer: Simon Borrough
Cartoon artwork: Richard Hook

First published in 1999 by Wayland Publishers Ltd, 61 Western Road,
Hove, East Sussex, BN3 1JD, England

British Library Cataloguing in Publication Data
Parsons, Martin
    Women's war. – (The history detective investigates. Britain at war)
    1. World War 1939–1945 – Women – Great Britain – Juvenile literature
    2. World War, 1939–1945 – War work – Great Britain – Juvenile literature
    3. World War, 1939–1945 – Participation, Female – Juvenile literature
    I. Title II. Hook, Richard
    941'.084'082
ISBN 0 7502 2312 X

Printed and bound in Italy by G. Canale & C SpA, Turin
Cover pictures: (bottom) land girls in 1941; (top-centre) a WVS badge; (top-right) a government
recruitment poster.
Title page: An air-raid warden and a nurse after an air raid.

Picture Acknowledgements: The publishers would like to thank the following for permission to
reproduce their pictures: Doreen Ellis 14 (top); E.T. Archives 27 (top); Hulton Getty Images *cover*
(bottom), *title page*, 6 (top), 8, 12 (top), 13, 14 (bottom), 15, 16 (bottom), 18 (right), 20 (top), 21
(bottom), 24 (right); Imperial War Museum, London 7 (bottom-right), 11 (left); John Frost
Historical Newspapers 25 (left); Peter Newark's Pictures 4 (bottom), 19 (bottom), 21 (top);
Popperfoto 5, 6 (bottom), 7 (top, bottom-left), 10 (top), 18 (left), 19 (top), 20 (bottom), 23, 24
(left), 27 (bottom), 29 (bottom); Press and Journal 4 (top); Public Record Office *cover* (top-right),
9, 10 (bottom), 16 (top), 22 (right), 29 (top); Robert Opie 12 (bottom); Science and Society
Picture Library 22 (left), 25 (right), 26, 28; Topham 17 (bottom); Wayland Picture Library
(photography by Rupert Horrox, courtesy of the Imperial War Museum, London) *cover* (top-left),
17 (top); Wayland Picture Library 11 (right). Logo artwork by John Yates.

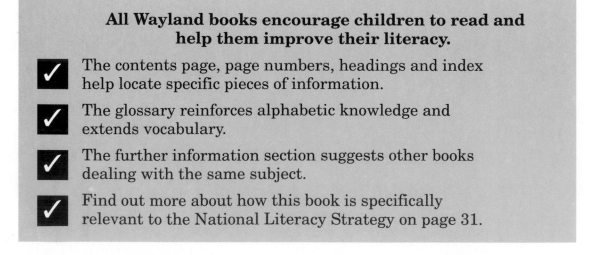

CONTENTS

WOMEN AT WAR

Members of the Women's Land Army at a fund-raising parade in February 1941.

A recruitment poster for the National Fire Service. Women did not fight fires, but worked as telephonists, despatch riders and cooks.

Before the Second World War, most women did not go out to work. Many people thought that a woman's proper role was to stay at home, looking after the children and doing the household chores. But when war broke out, men were conscripted into the armed forces. Women were now needed to do the jobs the men used to do. The lives of women would never be the same again.

For the first time, women were conscripted to help with the war effort. What kinds of job did they do? What was the Women's Land Army? How did women serve in the armed forces? There are many clues to tell us, if we only know where to look. By finding these clues, you can discover how women in your local area helped to win the war.

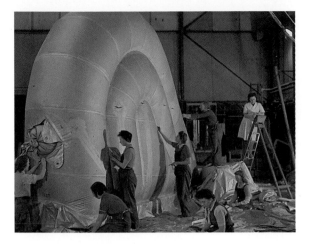

The history detective Shirley Bones will help you to find the clues you need. You should then be able to collect enough evidence and information to prepare and present your own project on women at war.

 Wherever you see one of Shirley's paw-prints, like this, you will find a mystery to solve. The answers can all be found on page 31.

The women in the photograph above are working in a factory in 1942. What do you think they are making? (You can find a big clue on page 28.)

A woman warden and medical officer join the search for survivors after an air raid.

DETECTIVE WORK

If you have female relatives who were adults at the time of the war, you could ask them about their experiences. This is called oral history, and it is an important way of gathering clues. Ask them if you can make a tape or even a video as they are talking. Try to find out how their lives changed during the war, and what kind of work they did.

FACTORY WORKERS

Between 1939 and 1943, 1.5 million women took jobs in 'essential industries' such as engineering, chemicals, gas, water, electricity, shipbuilding, aircraft production and munitions. Some working-class women had already been working in factories before the war, but for women from the middle and upper classes factory work was a new experience.

Cath and I went to see the wonderful munitions procession lining up in Hagley Road. It was to attract women to the factories. All firms sent contingents in marvellously coloured overalls on lorries containing parts of Spitfires, etc, with the words: *We Made These.*

Vere Hodgson, September 1941, in *Hearts Undefeated*

✿ Why do you think the workers in the procession described above wore coloured overalls?

Factory workers (right) in 1940, photographed taking their lunch break.

In March 1941, unmarried women between 20 and 30 were asked to register their current jobs with the local Employment Exchange. This meant they could be given suitable war work – which they had either done before, or could learn easily. The government could force women to take jobs or move to other ones. The files marked 'Council' at your local Record Office should contain letters from the government to local councils, telling them to conscript women for war work.

This worker is sharpening a saw in a steelworks in 1943.

Many women worked in munitions factories. The man in the photograph is probably the foreman.

DETECTIVE WORK
Visit your local reference library. Ask to use the microfilm viewer to look at wartime newspapers. You should be able to find advertisements trying to persuade women workers to take jobs in a particular industry. Shirley Bones has found one. Make copies of these adverts to use as illustrations in your project.

Women were paid less than men, and men in some industries felt that such cheap labour was a threat to their jobs. In many factories women workers faced practical problems, such as a lack of women's toilets. At the beginning of the war it was also very difficult for mothers to work in factories, because there were few nurseries to look after their children.

Women at work in a factory in 1944.

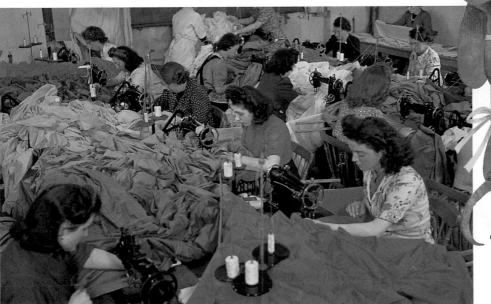

❖ What do you think the women in the two photographs on this page are making?

HOUSEWIVES

Women who went out to work played a vital role in the war effort, but women who stayed at home did an important job too. Housewives whose husbands were away fighting looked after their families in very difficult circumstances. By taking care of their neighbours' children, housewives also made it possible for many mothers to take jobs in the factories and voluntary services.

Wartime shortages meant that everyday tasks became a real challenge. Food was rationed, and housewives had to spend hours queuing for their share. They then had to find ways to make the rations stretch, so that everyone had enough to eat. This involved growing their own food, and coming up with new recipes to use what food was available.

Housewives also helped the war effort by recycling. Scrap metal, waste paper, rags and leftovers from meals were all recycled to make up for the many shortages caused by the war.

A housewife collecting scraps in 1940, to be recycled as pig food.

✿ Look carefully at the photograph on the left. What sort of scraps did the council want for recycling?

Clothing was rationed too. Women became expert at mending and altering garments, and also at making their own clothes. The government used adverts like the ones below to tell housewives how they could help the war effort. You may be able to find some by looking in old newspapers on microfilm at your local library.

An advertisement showing how needlework could help Britain to win the war.

🐾 What can be used to make a pair of slippers according to one of the headings in the advertisement above?

DETECTIVE WORK

Try to find clues such as ration books, wartime recipe books or books giving tips on how to 'make do and mend', by rummaging around in junk shops and at jumble sales and car-boot sales. These books can give you an idea of what everyday life was like for housewives during the war.

Although they worked very hard, some housewives worried that they were not doing enough. They felt guilty about staying at home. The government disagreed. In 1940, it even released a film, called *They Also Serve*, which showed how important the role of the housewife was to the war effort.

This advert asked people to save energy.

HOSTS

A host, Mrs Bryant, gives out clothes to evacuees living with her.

In 1939 and 1940, thousands of children were evacuated from areas that were likely to be bombed during German air raids. They travelled to places that the government thought would be safer. Women living in the safer areas did a very important job by offering homes to the evacuees. These women were known as hosts.

She's in the Ranks too!

CARING FOR EVACUEES IS A NATIONAL SERVICE

Evacuees' parents were supposed to pay for things like shoes and clothes. Some clothes were also donated by organizations such as the Women's Voluntary Service. However, many hosts used their own money to make life more comfortable for the children staying with them.

The poster on the left was issued by the Ministry of Health to show the importance of hosts.

✿ Who are hosts compared to in this poster?

The host in the photograph below, called Anne Norris, was awarded the British Empire Medal for looking after evacuees from London.

In Dorset, a Mrs Price took in seventeen evacuees. Although she received a lot of money for looking after the evacuees, her expenses must have been very high. Just think how long she must have spent in queues buying food for them all.

This poster called for more women to help with evacuees.

It was not only children who needed places to stay during the war. There were also many men and women in the armed forces living far from home, who needed billets. The newspaper cutting below is a vital clue telling us how much hosts were paid for giving board and lodging to soldiers of different ranks.

DORSET COUNTY CHRONICLE AND SWANAGE TIMES
7 September 1939

Soldier: Food and lodging 10d per night for one soldier, then 8d per night for others.

Officers, who would provide their own food: 3s per night for the first officer and then 2s a night for the others.

DETECTIVE WORK

Place a notice in your community newspaper or village magazine, asking women who looked after evacuees or other people during the war to write to you. Their letters about their experiences would be excellent documents to have in your project.

Dear Shirley, I have so many interesting things to tell you.....

🐾 If one ordinary soldier stayed at a house for 7 days, how much payment would the host receive? Remember, there were 12 pence (d) in every shilling (s).

TEACHERS

With so many men away fighting, there was a serious shortage of teachers. Women who had retired, or had given up teaching when they got married, were brought back to the classroom. Unfortunately, there was also a shortage of classrooms.

Evacuees from Rochester at a school in Sussex in 1941, having an outdoor lesson.

At Leiston school, for one session each day, we had the use of one small room which we and our evacuees had to share with a Dagenham headmistress. We had no apparatus, no guidance as to what to do or teach ... We gradually acquired a small collection of reading books, paper, pencils and crayons ... The rest of the school day we had to play in the park or walk the children around the lanes and go to the woods.

> Win Elliott and Sylvia Lewis, in *I'll Take That One*

Many teachers were evacuated with their schools. Like the children, they had to leave their homes and families behind and learn to live with strangers. They often had to teach in classrooms which were shared with other schools, or even outdoors.

Even an Oxo tin could start an invasion scare.

One teacher created an invasion scare when she organized a treasure hunt for her class. The children were given strict instructions to destroy all the clues once they had read them, but one was found by a villager. It simply said 'Go forward 500 yards to a gatepost near the cottage. Look for Oxo tin and follow instructions inside.' The local people thought it was the work of spies.

✿ What do you think the pupils in the photograph on the right are doing, and why? Shirley has found a clue.

Teachers acted as parents to many evacuees. They made sure that the children were being well looked after by their hosts, and checked whether they needed new shoes or clothes. Some gave up their Christmas and other holidays to stay in school, so that children who were feeling homesick could come and talk to them.

A teacher in 1940, taking a group of evacuees for a walk.

DETECTIVE WORK

If your school existed during the war, you might be able to find out who the teachers were at that time. You could put an appeal for information in the school newsletter or the local paper. Someone may even know where the teachers are living today, and you might be able to track them down. This is real detective work, and it is worth the trouble.

AIR-RAID WARDENS

Doreen Ellis, in 1999.

Every evening, air-raid wardens patrolled the streets making sure that no lights were showing during the blackout. If there was a bombing raid, the wardens guided people to shelters, set up first-aid posts and helped to rescue the injured.

Doreen Ellis was an air-raid warden in Maida Vale in north-west London. The following extracts are taken from an interview with her. She talks about her work during a heavy bombing raid on the night of 10 May 1942.

INTERVIEW WITH DOREEN ELLIS

The first thing we had to do after registering was to go out with a companion on 'lights' patrol, that was to check whether any light was showing on a certain patch. This particular evening a first-floor flat was showing a hall light. After finding out that there was no one in we found a ladder and climbed up to the first-floor balcony. We had to break in to turn off the light and then we left a note.

❖ Why was it important to make sure no lights were showing during an air raid?

INTERVIEW WITH DOREEN ELLIS

It was a very noisy night and we had several incidents and people coming in for shelter and first aid. About 1 am a doctor called in to help. I had difficulty in bandaging a knee and calf. I also put a tourniquet on a girl's wrist while out on patrol. She had passed out and I left her propped up sitting against a wall for an ambulance to pick up. She had a note on her good wrist saying who she was.

Doreen's story provides us with a lot of useful information about the work that wardens did. It helps us to imagine the effect the wardens' work had on their lives.

Rescuing a baby after an air raid in 1942.

Doreen's recollections of 10 May are very clear. She had recorded the events in her own diary, which is also a valuable source of clues.

Diary of Doreen Ellis

During this time several bombs had dropped. One sheered off a whole front of a block of flats and we had a steady stream of people coming in for shelter and first aid. A friend of mine was caught in the blast from a nearby bomb and was taken to hospital with many shrapnel wounds. The 'all-clear' went about 6 am and we were able to go home to bed, very weary. I got up at 8 am and went to work.

❧ What is shrapnel? You can find the answer somewhere in this book.

Imagine how exhausting it must have been to work through the night and then get up to do your normal job the next day.

DETECTIVE WORK

To create an interesting illustration for your project, take Doreen's account and make it into a strip cartoon. If you can find your own subject to interview, and then make it into a strip cartoon, that would be even better.

An air-raid warden and a nurse search for people trapped beneath rubble after an air raid.

VOLUNTEERS

Many women helped the war effort by doing voluntary work. The Women's Voluntary Service (WVS) was founded in 1938. By 1945, the WVS had over one million members.

A WVS recruitment poster.

Housewives!
W·V·S
needs your help!
Even if tied to your home you can help the wardens and your neighbours

A WVS mobile canteen. These canteens delivered refreshments to rescuers and survivors in areas damaged by bombing.

Voluntary workers were out on the streets every night during the Blitz, providing help and refreshments. Women working for the WVS set up mobile canteens to provide tea and sandwiches for exhausted rescue workers, victims of air raids, and people coming out of the shelters.

✿ Why do you think it was so important for the WVS to use mobile canteens, rather than setting up canteens in buildings?

> 4 am ... We open the side of the van, let down the counter, get the mugs from the drawers, by the light of a very small electric lamp. Then out of the darkness appear pale faces, the faces of men, women and children looking up at us. The sound of distant gunfire is drowned by coughing and a clamour of voices: 'Tea miss ... three teas, mate, and three nice cakes ...' From our van alone my colleague and I serve in under three hours about four hundred cups of tea.'
>
> Lorna Lewis, a worker in a mobile canteen, November 1940

Voluntary groups also helped combat war shortages. WVS members collected unwanted pots and pans, which could be melted down and recycled to make weapons and aircraft. They collected unwanted clothes, toys and household items to give to evacuees or to people who had lost everything in air raids. WVS knitting groups also made clothes and blankets to help keep these people warm in emergencies.

This badge was worn by the leader of a WVS group.

In the countryside, members of the Women's Institute (WI) were famous for making jam. They used fruit they had collected, and a special ration of sugar from the Ministry of Food. In 1940, five WI members in Kent with a canning machine produced 35 tonnes of canned fruit and 35 tonnes of jam.

A WVS knitting group in 1939. They met to knit clothes, and to make blankets out of squares of material. You can see one of these blankets on the table.

DETECTIVE WORK

If there is a WVS group in your area, write and ask where the minutes of wartime meetings are now kept. If you can get hold of these, you will be able to find out what your local group did during the war.

TRANSPORT WORKERS

After the introduction of conscription, there were not enough men to work in the vital areas of transport and communication. Before the war, few women had worked in these areas. Now they had to be quickly trained, in order to keep the country moving and to keep telephone switchboards working.

Many women were employed to operate the telephone switchboards at the centre of Britain's communications network. Others took on more unusual jobs as transport workers. Their tasks included driving tankers, and working as mechanics, railway guards and bus conductors. This was another example of women becoming accepted in jobs which before the war had been considered suitable only for men.

Mechanics (right) working on a petrol tanker in 1941.

This woman is acting as a signaller on a Yorkshire railway in 1941. She received only two weeks' training before she started her job.

> I. was troubled with uncertainty. Was it I who was going to dress up in conductor's uniform, run down to the tram depot in the blackout, shout 'Fares Please' [and] punch tickets ... Was this woman in navy blue myself?
>
> Zelma Katin,
> Clippie, The Autobiography of a Wartime Conductress, 1944

Women were fitted out with new uniforms, and quickly trained to work on the buses and trams. At first, women conductors seemed unusual, both to the passengers and to the conductresses themselves. Soon, though, nobody gave it a second thought.

Women bus conductors (right) working for London Transport in 1940.

A poster (below) advertising for bus and tram conductors.

By opening up new areas of employment and challenging the idea that women could not do certain jobs, the war changed life for women in Britain for ever.

DETECTIVE WORK

There are many transport museums around the country. Your local Tourist Information Centre should be able to help you find out if there are any near you. You could write to the museum, or visit, and try to find out what different transport jobs women took on in your area during the war.

LAND GIRLS

The Women's Land Army (WLA) was set up on 1 July 1939, and by 1943 there were 87,000 members. These women were known as 'land girls'. They successfully performed hard, physical work on the land, and provided Britain with vital supplies.

Land girls worked on farms, and in forests, nurseries and market gardens. They were usually given four or five weeks of basic training, although some were given no training at all. Some land girls worked with dairy cows. To learn how to milk them, they used bags full of water, hung from a frame. This training was vital, as the extract below explains.

A power cut meant that the whole dairy came to a standstill and the milking machines could not be used. All the men were called in to help with the hand-milking of forty cows. Here was where my milking training came in useful, the head cowman and myself being the only two people who had mastered the technique.

Dorothy Charlton in *Land Army Days: Cinderellas of the Soil*

This machine for teaching land girls how to milk cows was called 'Clarissa'.

Land girls worked very hard. Their tasks included ploughing, weeding, hoeing, muck-spreading, harvesting, digging ditches, trimming hedges, planting and digging up root vegetables, and looking after orchards. They worked long hours, and could take only one week's paid holiday a year. They were not given the same rights as women in the armed services, and the WLA became known as the 'Cinderella Service'.

Looking after lambs was one of the more enjoyable tasks for these land girls in 1943.

🐾 Why do you think the WLA was called the Cinderella Service?

> My white, tender hands were a thing of the past. Instead they became rough and calloused ... I rolled into bed at the end of the day to lay like a stone statue, not daring to move in case the pounding [backache] transferred itself all around my aching body.
>
> A. Ivy in *Land Army Days: Cinderellas of the Soil*

A recruitment poster (right) for the Women's Land Army.

✿ How is the image of a land girl shown in the poster different from the reality shown in the black-and-white photograph below and described in the document on the left?

Land girls, the Giles sisters, being instructed by the farmer who employed them in 1942.

'We could do with thousands more like you..'

JOIN THE WOMEN'S LAND ARMY

DETECTIVE WORK

At your local reference library, use the microfilm reader to look in wartime newspapers for articles about the Land Army. You might also find advertisements for equipment and clothing for land girls.

SERVICE LIFE –
BEHIND THE SCENES

Separate branches of the army, navy and air force were set up for women to join. The Auxiliary Territorial Service (ATS) was the women's branch of the army. Women who wished to join the air force signed up with the Women's Auxiliary Air Force (WAAF). Those who preferred the navy applied to the Women's Royal Naval Service (WRNS), and were known as Wrens.

This recruitment poster was designed to show that a driver's job with the ATS could be glamorous.

Ceaselessly new vehicles roll off the production lines. Army units await them, the ATS deliver them

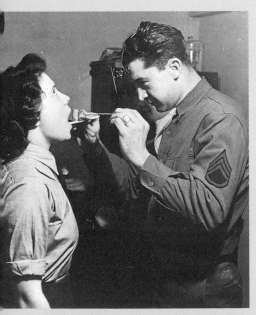

A WAAF officer is given a medical by an American officer in 1942. Many WAAFs worked with the US forces stationed in Britain.

When the war began, most women in the services worked as cooks and clerks. Some worked in operations rooms as telephone operators and 'plotters'. Plotters in the WAAF moved markers on a large map to show the approach of enemy bombers.

😾 Why do you think members of the Women's Royal Naval Service were known as Wrens?

> The plotter moves her billiard cue again, and the counter approaches closer to our coast ... a WAAF telephone operator moves a switchboard plug, a message goes back to Command, and a few minutes later the siren wails in some coastal town. For that was the birth of an air-raid warning, in an operations room many miles from the raided town, and it was a WAAF officer who gave the word that set the sirens going.
>
> Elspeth Huxley, WAAFS in the Operation Room, July 1942,
> quoted in Hearts Undefeated

You can see the plotter at work on her ladder in this photograph of a wartime operations room.

😾 How do we know that this photograph was taken in, or after, 1940? (The clue is in the text on this page.)

Wrens also worked as plotters, to show the movement of naval ships and merchant convoys. At one command centre, in Liverpool, the map was on the wall and the plotters had to climb tall ladders to move the markers. In 1940, a Wren fell off and was killed. After that date, plotters all had to wear parachute harnesses hanging from the ceiling. You can still visit the command centre where the Wren's ghost is supposed to haunt the room.

DETECTIVE WORK

Look up the Army, Navy or Royal Air Force in the telephone directory. Find the address of its information office. Write and ask for information about women who served in the forces in your local area in the Second World War.

SERVICE LIFE – WOMEN IN ACTION

The role of women in the armed forces caused many arguments. People felt that the actual fighting should be left to the men. However, as the war went on, more and more service women performed roles that were close to the action.

Despatch riders at a training centre in 1943.

Women in the ATS took on many jobs. Some became mechanics, drivers and motorcycle despatch riders. Others worked as welders, carpenters and electricians. Women on the anti-aircraft sites perhaps came closest to fighting. Some directed searchlights at enemy bombers. Others prepared the anti-aircraft guns – but they were not allowed to fire them.

ATS women operating searchlights. Their job was to light up enemy bombers in the dark so that anti-aircraft guns could be fired at them.

Officers were instructed never to allow anything that would cause public outcry. Girls on the batteries were all volunteers, but if their parents objected they were posted elsewhere.

Leslie Whateley, director of the ATS

A recruitment poster for the WAAF.

Some women in the WAAF were trained as flight mechanics, but very few of them actually flew. Those that did transported Spitfires, Hurricanes and other aircraft from the factories where they were made, to the airfields where they were needed. Some women pilots transported large bomber planes. But the majority of women in the forces had to make the best of less exciting jobs.

✿ What do the words of the poster on this page tell us about the different roles of men and women?

DETECTIVE WORK

Look through the local telephone directory, and try to find any local army, navy or air force museums. Telephone or visit the museums, and try to find out as much information as you can about women in the forces. See if there are any postcards for sale which could be used to illustrate your project.

A pilot in 1940. Her job was to transport aircraft from the factories to the airfields.

NURSES

Extra nurses were needed to deal with the many wartime emergencies. Nurses had to work under very dangerous conditions. Some became service nurses, working abroad for the armed forces in military hospitals near battlefields. Others worked in British hospitals. They treated the injuries and illnesses caused by air raids, blackouts and wartime shortages.

Nurses at home and abroad worked in 'casualty clearing stations'. Here, the injured were given emergency treatment until they could be transferred to hospitals. The document below gives us an idea of the conditions nurses faced each day.

Nurses during gas mask training in 1939.

The men were lying in such a variety of positions, often with their limbs stuck out at queer angles in the plaster splints or sometimes slung on frames and hung with weights and pulleys; the light caught the glass flasks of blood which was still dripping slowly into the four bad cases.

Lena K. Chivers, a nurse at a casualty clearing station in August 1944, quoted in *Hearts Undefeated*

DETECTIVE WORK

Some large houses in the countryside were used as convalescence homes, where injured people were sent once they had started to get better. Visit your local Record Office and find out if there were any of these convalescence homes near you. Look up 'Convalescence Homes' under 'Wartime'. The archivist will help you.

Nurses on motorized bicycles called 'autocycles', in 1939.

During a bombing raid a hospital was just as likely to be hit as any other building. Some nurses found themselves working in operating theatres where the electricity kept going off and the ceiling was falling in around them. Between 1940 and 1942, 15 nurses were awarded George Medals for their bravery.

Of course, nurses still had to look after people with everyday illnesses. They also carried out health checks on evacuees. District nurses travelled from house to house, looking after people who were not sick enough to be in hospital. Many travelled by motorcycle or bicycle. They rode in the darkness of the blackout along roads littered with rubble from bombed buildings.

A George Medal, awarded for bravery.

🐾 Why would wartime nurses have travelled by motorcycle and not by car?

YOUR PROJECT

These service women in 1941 are tying down a barrage balloon. These balloons were floated high into the sky to prevent German bombers from flying low over their targets.

If you have been following the detective work at the end of each section, you should have found plenty of clues. These clues will help you to produce your own project about the lives of women in Britain during the Second World War.

Women were involved in many different aspects of the war, so you first need to choose a topic which interests you. You could use one of the questions below as a starting point.

Topic Questions
- How did women in the countryside help with the war effort?
- What was a day in the life of a land girl like?
- How did government posters portray women?
- How did voluntary workers help victims of air raids?
- What was it like to be a nurse in wartime?

When you have gathered all your information, think of an interesting way to present it. You might like to use one of the ideas below.

A government recruitment poster for women workers.

> ## Project Presentation
> - Collect all the cuttings, advertisements and photographs you have found and produce your own newspaper.
> - Write your project in the form of a diary.
> - Produce a video or poster to encourage people to volunteer for war work.
> - Divide your project into two halves, showing the contrast between women before and after the outbreak of war.

You might find an unusual subject for your topic. Shirley Bones found that some women helped to keep up morale during the war by entertaining people. There were female singers, musicians and comedians, who toured the country giving shows to troops and workers. Shirley even found a photograph of an ATS dance band.

An ATS dance band in 1944.

GLOSSARY

armed forces The army, navy and air force.

auxiliaries Workers who play a supporting role.

billets Accommodation, for soldiers or evacuees, in civilian houses.

blackout A period during the hours of darkness when no lights were allowed to be used.

Blitz The air raids launched by German bombers against Britain from 1940 to 1941.

calloused Hardened, for example where skin on the hands has been hardened by work.

civilian Not in the armed forces.

conductor/conductress Someone who collects fares and checks tickets on a bus or tram.

conscripted Forced to take part in wartime service.

contingents Particular groups, for example in an army or in a parade.

despatch riders Riders who carry important letters and messages.

evacuated Moved to an area of safety.

foreman A worker who supervises others.

merchant convoys Groups of ships carrying goods such as food and fuel.

minutes The official record of a meeting.

mobilized Prepared and put into action during a war or emergency.

munitions Military equipment, especially ammunition.

operations room A room where officers control military operations.

rationed Restricted, so that people can only have a certain amount each week.

shrapnel Small, sharp fragments scattered by a bomb, which can cause terrible injuries.

switchboard A system in a telephone exchange where calls are connected by hand.

tourniquet A tight bandage which stops the flow of blood.

tram A bus powered by electric cables which runs on rails through a city.

voluntary services Organizations run by volunteers, such as the WVS.

BOOKS TO READ

Hearts Undefeated edited by Jenny Hartley (Virago, 1994) This is a wonderful collection of women's writing from the Second World War.

I'll Take That One by Martin Parsons (Becket Karlson, 1999)

Quiet Heroines: Nurses of the Second World War by Brenda McBryde (Cakebreads, 1989)

Raiders Overhead: A Diary of the London Blitz by Barbara Nixon (Scolar/Gulliver 1980)

Wartime Women, edited by Dorothy Sheridan (Mandarin, 1991)

Children can use this book to improve their literacy skills in the following ways:

✓ To identify the many different types of text, and to understand the use of fact and opinion (Year 4, Term 1, Non-fiction reading comprehension).

✓ To use the Detective Work panels to prepare for factual research by reviewing what is known, what is needed and where to search (Year 4, Term 2, Non-fiction reading comprehension).

✓ To identify the features of a recounted text, comparing the air-raid warden's diary with her oral recollections (Year 5, Term 1, Non-fiction reading comprehension).

✓ To evaluate government advertisements for their impact, appeal and honesty (Year 4, Term 3, Non-fiction reading comprehension).

Puzzle Answers

Page 5:

❖ The women are making barrage balloons. These balloons were used to make enemy aircraft fly higher and so make it more difficult for them to bomb targets accurately.

Page 6:

❖ Coloured overalls gave the impression that their jobs and working conditions were attractive and exciting.

Page 7:

❖ The women in the top photograph are making hand grenades. Those in the bottom photograph are making parachutes.

Page 8:

❖ The council wanted scraps from vegetables, salads, meat, fish and bread, plus potato and apple peel. They did not want tea, coffee, the skins of grapefruit, oranges, lemons and bananas, or rhubarb tops. (Rhubarb tops make pigs very ill!)

Page 9:

❖ Slippers could be made out of an old felt hat.

Page 10:

❖ The advert compares hosts to people in the armed forces, showing that hosts have an equally important part to play in winning the war.

Page 11:

❖ The soldier would pay: 10d x 7 days = 70d. Divide this by 12 to convert into shillings and the answer is 5s 10d.

Page 13:

❖ The children are being shown how to darn their socks. Clothes were rationed, so it was important to learn how to mend old clothes.

Page 14:

❖ Lights could be seen from the air by bomber pilots, which made it easier for them to hit their targets.

Page 15:

❖ Shrapnel is the name given to metal pieces of bombs, which travel at high speed after a bomb explodes, killing and injuring many people. You can find this information in the glossary.

Page 16:

❖ Mobile canteens could deliver refreshments to the areas where they were most needed. Also, there was always the danger that canteens in buildings might be destroyed by bombing.

Page 20:

❖ It was called the Cinderella Service because the women often worked long hours in poor conditions without getting any thanks – just like the fairy-tale character.

Page 21:

❖ The poster makes the land girls' life look very clean, easy and comfortable. The photograph shows how dirty the job could be in bad weather – the land girls have clearly been working in mud. The document tells us how hard land girls worked.

Page 23:

❖ They were known as Wrens because the name of the women's navy was shortened to WRNS.

❖ We know the photograph was taken after 1940 because the plotter is wearing a parachute harness. As the main text tells us, plotters only wore harnesses after one of them fell to her death in 1940.

Page 25:

❖ The poster uses words which reveal that men will be in the action while women will play supporting roles. These words are 'Serve in the WAAF, with the men who fly'.

Page 27:

❖ Travelling by motorcycle or bicycle used less petrol – which was rationed because it was in short supply.

INDEX

Numbers in **bold** refer to pictures and captions.

AWARD WINNING! **woman** 1984 26p —EXTRA Special!

EXCLUSIVE MARIE HELVIN The most moving photo-session of her life

Big steps in the life of little PRINCE WILLIAM

FREE INSIDE

Delightful PRINCESS DIANA Poster/Calendar

PLUS! 84's ZIPPIEST IN AND OUT GUIDE

Over-indulged? Our NEW YEAR DIET PLAN will knock lots off you.

VOGUE

shameless escape from all this to all that

from now to summer new looks in fashion make-up accessories

health '75 new exercise diet keep-fit plan

vogue talent contest '75

FAIRLADY

WIN R2500 in fashion prizes plus fragrance and an opal and diamond ring

CHARLES AND DIANA —their home sweet homes and married bliss

FREE French Cookery School Part 8

Harpers & Queen APRIL 1977 ★ 60p

GOD SAVE THE PRINCESS OF WALES! Nigel Dempster on the real one

BEAUTY JOINS THE SPACE AGE

VOGUE JUNE 35p

fashion, jewels, scent, that make up the best looks now

invest in YOUR SELF

diet, exercise, cosmetic surgery, the good-health vitamin/mineral hormone

---

Harpers & Queen DECEMBER 1978 35p

EVERYTHING YOU COULD WANT FOR CHRISTMAS: PRESENTS WITH PRESENCE AND HOT

SOCIAL CLIMBING AND SOCIAL PLUNGING

FINER FOOD FINER WINE

TESTING THE NEW COOKERY BOOKS

PLUS PRINCE CHARLES GRACE JONES ARTHUR MILLER FRAN LEBOWITZ PHILIPPE de ROTHSCHILD TINA CHOW BUBBLES ROTHERMERE MIRO SYBILLE BEDFORD

AND WE KNOW THE SECRETS OF THE BLACK (MAGIC) BOX

COSMOPOLITAN October 1976 • 30p

At Home With The Oil Sheikhs. An Extract from Linda Blandfords Probing New Book

Is Too Much Sexual Freedom Undermining Your Relationship?

Flexitime: How to Beat the Nine-to-Five Rat Race with This Civilised New Way to Work

The Case for Marrying a Younger Man

How to Cope With Obscene Telephone Calls

Breaking Up With a Man. How to Get Through Those First Days and Nights, by Anna Raeburn

Put a Message in a Bottle. You Could Win a Fabulous Holiday for Two on a Tropical Island

Piers Paul Reads Surprising Love Story: Polonaise. Plus an Extract from the Crazy Sex-comedy Kinflicks

---

VOGUE FEB 50p

NEWS IN COLOUR WHAT TO WEAR WITH WHAT NOW

NEWS IN BEAUTY, HAIR, HEALTH

NEWS FROM THE SCHOOL MAGAZINES

NEWS IN FASHION AT A PRICE YOU CAN AFFORD

NEWS FROM THE SEX REVOLUTION

VOGUE ITALIA

IN "VISTAVISION" DA TAHITI LA COLORATA MODA MARE '76

SENTIRSI IN FORMA TUTTA L'ESTATE

• con le divise degli atleti
• con la dieta vegetariana
• con una settimane in una fattoria della bellezza

MARIE HELVIN

Catwalk

THE ART OF MODEL STYLE

PAVILION
MICHAEL JOSEPH

First published in Great Britain
in 1985 by Pavilion Books Limited
196 Shaftesbury Avenue, London WC2H 8JL
in association with Michael Joseph Limited
44 Bedford Square, London WC1B 3DP

Text © 1985 Marie Helvin

Designed by Lawrence Edwards
Edited by Vicky Hayward
Co-ordinated by Lucinda Montefiore

Helvin, Marie
    Catwalk: the art of model style
    1. Helvin, Marie 2. Models, Fashion – Great Britain –
    Biography
    1. Title
    659.1'52   HD6073.M772G7

    ISBN 0-907516-64-5

Printed and bound in Italy by Arnoldo Mondadori

CONTENTS

Acknowledgements

I would not have been able to write this book without the help and support of many colleagues and friends. First and foremost, I would like to thank David Bailey, without whose generosity and help the book simply would not have been possible.

For their help with practical information on hair and skin care, exercise and cosmetics, I am indebted to John Frieda, Leslie Kenton, Dreas Reyneke, Paul Gobel and Della Finch, who all gave their time and invaluable knowledge. Within the modelling profession, Jerry Hall, Iman, Pat Cleveland, Ines de la Fressange, Jane Massey and Catrina Skepper all passed on to me ideas and experiences. The section for models who are starting out was compiled with the help of Monique Pillard at Elite Model Management, New York, José Fonseca at Models One, Laraine Ashton and Sara Dukas. Grace Coddington of British Vogue, Alex Kroll at Condé Nast, Gianni Versace and Maxine Van Cliffe were also very kind with their help at various points.

Many other people, too numerous to mention, have helped along the way. However, I would like to thank Sara Preston and Adrian Paul, and the friends who have carried me through with their support – especially Tina Chow, Loulou de la Falaise, Manolo Blahnik, Bruce Oldfield, Sara Giles, Nadia and Suomi La Valle and, of course, the Lee Helvin clan. Most of all, however, it was left to Mark to calm me, cajole me and help me laugh when the going got rough.

Finally, I would like to thank my publisher, Colin Webb. This book has been a long time in the making and he has shown great patience and faith in the project from beginning to end.

For Suzon Lee Helvin
Me Ke Aloha Pumehana

A CHILD OF THE ISLANDS

My father taught me from the time we were knee-high that there were three golden rules to life: never to accept anything at face value, never to succumb to blind obedience, and to remember that while I owed first allegiance to myself, my family and those I loved, I was also a child of the world. He later added a more pragmatic piece of advice: take advantage of any opportunities that come your way.

Pop, who is of French and Danish extraction, was brought up in Virginia, spoke like a real Southerner and christened us all with the same second name, Lee, in honour of the Confederate General. My mother grew up in the mountainous region of Hokkaido, the northernmost island of Japan, originally the land of the albino Ainu people who are thought by some to be descendants of Genghis Khan. Her childhood was extraordinary. Raised by one of her sisters, because it was considered shameful that my grandmother had given birth at the age of fifty-five, she only learned the identity of her true mother when she was seventeen. A woman of many talents, she had won a scholarship to study opera in Italy, but had not been allowed by her family to take up the place, and had been working as an interpreter in the American officers' club in Sapporo when she met my father, then a GI.

The match was, perhaps rather surprisingly, approved by my mother's family, largely through a tragic quirk of fate. They felt it would balance the sadness of their son's death; he had been prevented by the war from marrying the American girl he loved and had then been killed in action. My parents at first lived in Tokyo, where I was born, however because of the ongoing Korean War they felt it would be safer to return to America. They finally settled in Washington, D.C., because it was one of the most cosmopolitan and open-minded American cities at that time. Here my two sisters, Suzon and Naomi, were born. Then we uprooted again, first to Honolulu and then back to Tokyo, where we spent several happy years before deciding to make Hawaii our home. I was just eight years old when we returned there by ship.

My most vivid childhood memory is my first glimpse of Honolulu on that journey. Standing on the ship's deck with my two sisters and one of the stewards, I suddenly noticed a cluster of mysterious bright lights glittering in the distance. Fascinated, I asked the steward if he knew what they could be. He had seen the sense of magic in my eyes and, not wishing to break the spell, he told me that everyone in Hawaii had switched on their house lights to welcome us. I was overcome by a sense of pure enchantment that I never experienced again.

The memory of that moment remained to infuse my childhood with a sense of wonder and the belief that Hawaii was a place of special qualities and powers. I was a true child of the islands: my greatest treat was to be taken once a year, in November, to the outlying island of Maui to watch the humpback whales frolicking in the bay where they came to give birth. Other pleasures were less rare. During the summer holidays my sisters and I would often get up before dawn and cycle with our breakfasts to a large tree, where we would perch, munching toast, steeped in a sense of paradise as we watched the sun flooding the sky with spectacular, sometimes almost garish, colours. In the wet season I would go out with friends to Jackass Ginger, a rocky slope in the mountains which would become a natural water chute after a hard rain, and coast down over the stones on a mat woven from ti-leaves until I was defeated by the bumps and bruises on my bottom.

As I grew older, I came to look on these and other everyday pleasures, like the heady scent of frangipani, the luxury of walking barefoot, the rainbow-hued skies and the balmy evenings, as incomparable privileges.

As a child, I was never aware that my mixed blood might be considered exotic or unusual because Hawaii is such a glorious chop suey of races and many of my friends were *hapa-haole*, or half-white, with varying proportions of Chinese, Japanese, Filipino or Hawaiian blood. I was equally unaware that it could be considered unusual to have parents of different nationalities. Since my mother never made a great fuss about preserving her native ways within the family and Hawaii had by then become the fiftieth state of the Union, my adolescence bore a strong resemblance to that of any West Coast beach baby and so I tended to see myself as an American and gave very little thought to my oriental side.

As the eldest of four children (my little brother was born in Hawaii) I saw myself as the protective elder sister, the conciliator who arbitrated when squabbles broke out. How they saw me, I am not so sure. There were allegations of bossiness. When I was older and my parents went away – as they did about three times a year to escape from us all – I was always left to look after the brood. Once there was a tidal wave alert – a moment of real fear in Hawaii since the last big wave, in 1960, had killed sixty-one people who had been watching it sweep in from a bridge. We lived on high ground so I saw no reason to leave the house, which led my little brother to accuse me of trying to kill them. In fact, he could only be calmed by giving him our greatest family treat – bouncing barefoot on my father's favourite chair.

I was closest to Suzon, the elder of my two sisters, from whom I learned a lot, even as a child. She was beautiful, very funny, but also sensitive and vulnerable, and as a result was mercilessly teased at high school by the local *tiida's*, a gang of tough Hawaiian and Samoan girls, whose taunts I bought off by bribing the ringleader with cigarettes. Our younger sister, Naomi, was very different. Quite capable of giving as good as she got, honest and with a very forthright tongue, she was a headstrong girl, but also had a gentler side and was an endless source of fun. Steve, my little brother, was young enough to be cute rather than a pest. When I was older, it became a Friday night ritual for me to take him to the drive-in. A look of barely hidden horror would come over some of my dates' faces when they discovered that a five-year-old chaperone was a part of the deal. He was never any trouble. Curled up in the back seat in a little nest hollowed out of blankets, he would down a bag of popcorn in the intermission and then, as regular as clockwork, fall asleep half way through the main movie.

My parents, each in their own way, instilled in me a rare sense of values. Pop was a true Southern gentleman, but also an idealist of unorthodox beliefs tempered by a terrific sense of humour. At one stage, when I was

Early poses, graduating from the chubby chipmunk through the Mickey Mouse club years to the self-conconscious stringbean on Waikiki Beach (right). Mom was sporting Honolulu's answer to the coolie hat; Suzon and I were pretending to model stockings; Naomi and Steve were still ignorant of fashion. Far right: Several years on, with mom and pop, still my greatest fans.

about fourteen and America was at the height of its paranoia of the Red bomb, he announced that he thought we should all move to New Zealand to avoid obliteration. Fortunately his plan for us to sit on a beach in peace living off canned beans came to nothing because we all protested so loudly. In fact we did not even get a fallout shelter. Never a man for half-measures, Pop built a patio instead.

On the spiritual side, he was equally open-minded, having suffered a strict Baptist upbringing, and encouraged us to give every creed equal consideration rather than mindlessly say our prayers and trot off to church. After I left home, he moved over to Buddhism, which rested on his shoulders more naturally than Christianity. A child of the Depression years and an independent businessman, he was also determined that we should not grow up into spoilt brats: he expected us to earn our weekly allowance through work around the house and always made it clear that we would be expected to earn our own living as soon as we left school. Some of my friends thought he was a little weird, partly because he was very excitable, but mainly because he was a dedicated health and exercise nut long before the age of mass vegetarianism and work-outs – he would force watercress and carrot juice down us at breakfast and line his skinny daughters up for weight training. I rebelled against this and by the age of fourteen was downing beer by the six-pack and puffing away at cigarettes, but his general message had hit home and I always knew that looking good also meant looking after my body.

My mother was quite different by temperament. A calm but very spirited woman who was constantly bubbling over with laughter, she told me when I was older how difficult America had been at first, not simply because of the anti-Japanese feelings which lingered after the war, but also

the small-town hospitality and social etiquette. She went through agonies dealing with tea-bags at polite coffee mornings – my father swears that she ate the first one that confronted her. In fact it took her a long time to work out how coffee deserved a written invitation in the first place. I could never have guessed this as a child: she had so wholeheartedly embraced Americanism that oriental values were rarely evident in her attitudes. We kept only one Japanese tradition, that of the annual boys' and girls' day, but even this had been completely transformed to a Helvin-style children's holiday. Every few months we could each have our parents to ourselves for the day and choose exactly what we could do with them.

Mom treated all her children as friends and always encouraged our independence and freedom, but she could be quite strict if she considered it necessary, although in a very gentle way. If we were standing in the kitchen, she used to vent her annoyance when I had been caught cutting class by breaking an egg over my head – a deliciously sensuous punishment – until the unhappy day when she discovered me afterwards using it to act out a commercial for hair conditioner to the bathroom mirror. I inherited from her a great respect for generosity of spirit, gentleness and lack of vanity.

At one stage this developed into a rather curious reverence for my notion of saintly womanhood. I revered the nuns at the Star of the Sea, the local Catholic church, and for several years I would run down after school to ask if I could carry their books for them. This fascination became mixed up with my childish admiration of pretty women, which provided a series of strange childhood heroines: the healthy wench with the peasant blouse and basket of grapes on the Sunmaid raisin packet, Gina Lollobrigida as Esmeralda in *The Hunchback of Notre Dame*, and Jennifer Jones, the clean-faced virgin in *The Song of Bernadette*. This innocent faith in the power of goodness led me to believe that the people I cared for led a charmed existence.

That sense of a safely protected world was shattered by Vietnam. It is hard to explain to people who did not grow up close to the war, in terms of geographical proximity, age bracket or the involvement of one's government, what an extraordinary strength of feeling and sense of questioning it produced in a generation of hearts and minds. Most of my friends reacted very strongly against Vietnam: after all, we were very close to the war as Honolulu was both a major command headquarters and one of the rest and recreation centres where GIs were sent as a reward when their battalions had good killing scores. For a time we talked of little else, both in and out of class, and at home. Early evenings were dominated by the six o'clock news and the clinical roll-call of casualties and deaths.

The futile and senseless violence shown by the newsreels imprinted on my mind indelible images of terror and pain: the self-immolation of the young Buddhist monk, Tet Kuan Duk, in 1966, his slight body consumed by tongues of flame in the streets of Saigon. His fate symbolized his people's innocent suffering, the lotus sacrificed to the fire. Nor can I forget the faces of young GIs fixing to die: running into battle, brutalized by the Mylai massacre, mutilated by a sniper's grenade. The expressions on their faces told more powerfully than any words of the chasm that separated them from the folks back home. Deeply disturbed, and encouraged by my father, I marched in protest against the draft, chanting anti-war slogans, and planned to become a peace worker. Later, when I had great problems obtaining a passport, the only plausible explanation I could find was the CIA surveillance of those protest marches.

I was always very proud to be a kamaaina, or old-timer, Hawaiian, and loved returning home to leis and guava jam, ukelele music and the hula. I had learnt the hula as a child and would practise the hand movements in bed at night, watching the shadows on the wall. Both these pictures were taken on one of my visits home from Japan.

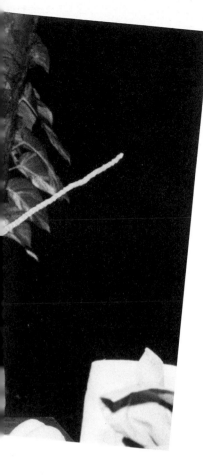

Apart from this my high school years were very carefree. Hawaiian life is so relaxed, its ways so uninhibited. We lived with little or no care for punctuality, and nobody worried if I came home late; in fact I spent more time on the beach than at home. I grew up in a bikini – even wearing it under my school clothes – and every day I would go to Sandy Beach or another hot surf spot with my girlfriends. We would lounge around drinking beer and getting stoned, listening to surf reports on the radio and waxing our guys' boards.

When I was twelve or thirteen I had my first kiss, with a boy called Billy from the Salvation Army Home. Billy was a naughty boy and I knew exactly what he wanted when he asked me to go outside at Skateland one evening. The kiss was great, way beyond expectations, and when Mom picked me up she kept asking why I had a smile the width of my face. (I did not tell her the reason.) Now, unfortunately, Skateland has become the Honolulu Pathological Institute and I get the creeps instead of happy nostalgia every time I pass it. My second kiss was not so good. It was in a little hidden chamber in a huge man-made pool filled with sea water. There was just enough air to breathe and kiss, but we got caught as the tide was coming in and we had a terrible struggle to get out before our lungs ran out of air. Survival instinct replaced any sentimentality; he kicked me in the neck and I knew I was close to drowning.

Parties were another favourite occupation. At first these were known as making-out parties, which were little more than innocent kissing sessions to music, with discussion about technique between the girls in the kitchen, and fighting between the boys in the yard. These were held wherever parents had gone out for the evening, although they were pretty innocuous; whenever I thought there was a risk of my sofa life getting too hot I would invisibly safety-pin the zip on my jeans. Some girls were known to 'put out', but I certainly did not approve. My first boyfriend, a blue-eyed, blond beachbum called Ken who went on to become a surf champion, was considered the catch of the school, but after a couple of months I had the bad taste to drop him and he was followed by a series of instantly forgettable names ending with a worthless hunk of beefcake called Russell.

My parents were pretty easy-going about boys. When they went away, I would always hold an all-night party with an enormous pot of stew made from every can in the cupboard and a dollar's worth of ice from the gas station in the trash can for the beer that everyone was expected to bring along. My baby brother and sisters remained curiously unimpressed by all this, and one morning, cycling back from a tree breakfast, Suzon gave me a few strong words. I had apparently become very boring, interested in boys and dating all the time instead of having fun with them. Now I think she was probably right. At the time, I thought it meant I had stopped being a child.

With maturity came be-ins and love-ins. These were basically making-out parties dressed up with long discussions about Woodstock and Carlos Castaneda, psychedelic rock and assorted drugs. There were always plenty of those. We were very American in our tastes, although desperately aware of being country cousins. I remember my outrage when Mick Jagger asked the radio reporter off-handedly where he had landed when the Rolling Stones came to Honolulu, and by the end of high school, I was desperate to get off the rock for a look at the world of my heroes.

But, for all my supposedly grown-up ideas, I was still very naive. I totally lacked confidence in myself and I suffered agonies about my braces, glasses and flat chest; self-contempt, not narcissism, lay behind my stolen glances into mirrors. I longed for a curvy bikini figure, firmly believing, as I was told by every teenage magazine, that a Monroe-style cleavage was necessary to get the right boyfriend. But I remained so underdeveloped, especially in comparison to all my friends who had gone on the Pill, that I hated getting undressed after sports at school, let alone being seen in my bikini by the surfboys. I was not to find my confidence for many years, but I did come to realize its importance while I was still at school. This happened in a curious way. I chanced on a quasi-religious self-help book, with some thoroughly cheapskate title like *How To Be A Success*, in the school library when I had been sent out of the maths class. A more sophisticated teenager would probably have dismissed it – even I found the title a little suspect – but once I had opened it and read that I might be able to change the course of my life simply by altering my attitudes, I was riveted. The considerate author had even given practical techniques to follow, which, when detached from the label they were given – visualization imagery – boiled down to taking a well-thought-out strategical approach rather than collapsing at the first hurdle, which was my usual reaction to obstacles.

I stole the book and when I got home I read it from cover to cover, sitting up late into the night. Laughable as it may sound, that book quite literally changed my life. From that day on I began to assess myself realistically and to search within myself, instead of looking to props around me, for the sense of purpose and the faith in my own judgment I needed to realize my daydreams. When I left Hawaii a year later the book went with me, and remained by my side for many years.

I left home for the first time shortly after graduation, but only for a short

Left: The Hawaiian hippy look, as I launched it in Tokyo on my first visit. I think I left the plumeria flower behind.

Right: Campaign posters as the Kanebo girl including my first ever shot for a Christmas advertisement and a less sickly sweet sequence shot in Death Valley, California. By this time, the chipmunk cheeks had disappeared, but the teeth were still in evidence.

holiday, expecting to return for a spell of beach life, followed possibly by college, since I was at the time seized by the idea of studying oceanography. I visualized this as a curious amalgam of books, beach life and a leisurely look at the marine life of the islands. One evening, shortly after the glorious freedom of my final day at high school, my father presented me with a double ticket to Tokyo, explaining characteristically that this was to be my graduation present because it would be far more valuable for me to visit with my mother the country where I had been born than to own a gold watch.

It was an extraordinary first glimpse of the world outside. The smallest details impressed me: the pre-packed food on the airplane, the view of the Imperial Palace from our hotel bedroom and, perhaps most of all, the brightly painted taxis, which I mistook as the last word in psychedelic car decoration. My only real disappointments were, firstly, the dirtiness of the air and, secondly, the men, who seemed pretty paltry specimens measured against the Hawaiian surf boys. I was also made to feel acutely self-conscious about my own appearance. The Japanese never seemed to stop staring at me in a curious, highly embarrassing way. I suppose I must have looked like a crazed giant from a banana boat to the neat, conservatively fashionable Tokyo women, with their regulation handbags and stockings, especially since I wandered around with my untamed hair curling down my back and the briefest of mini-skirts.

Shortly before we were due to leave, a very elegant woman came up to me in the hotel coffee shop and asked whether I was a model. I explained that I was a student, and she asked whether I would like to visit a company she represented, called Kanebo, to discuss the possibility of modelling for a range of cosmetics. After she and my mother had chatted for a while and discovered that they had mutual friends, I agreed, mainly because my mother seemed keen for me to show interest. To my astonishment, they offered me, that very afternoon, a three-year contract worth thousands of dollars.

It was a strange experience to discover overnight that I might be considered a beauty, and, furthermore, that my looks could be worth so much to me financially. Of course, I had been conscious of my looks and figure, just like any teenage girl, but my self-image had always been that of a gawky, flat-chested string bean with a frizzy mass of hair. And the length of my legs, which was now being treated as a valuable asset, had before always been a liability, getting tangled underneath me when I played soccer and making my skirt look so short that I was constantly being sent home from school, despite my parents' untiring explanations that it was not the skirt, but the legs, which were the root of the problem.

Most astonishing of all was the idea that I had been picked out for my face. Suzon had always been the beauty of the family. One year I reached the height of my pre-teen ambitions and became the May Day Queen at school, and another time got myself into *Young Hawaii*, the hip Honolulu kids' fashion magazine, wearing the latest beach look. But I spent most of my high school years trying to overcome what I considered my shortfall on looks by covering my face with white powder to look startling and weird. Occasionally I would idly browse through fashion magazines if I was waiting for my mother at the hairdressers, but never dared to dream of the world of the glossy cover-girl.

So, although I was tremendously flattered by Kanebo's offer, I turned it down without much heart-searching. Although modelling sounded very glamorous and the contract represented untold riches, I had never seriously considered that kind of life style, and I was a little doubtful about the prospects. I also felt scared by the outcome of taking such a hurried decision. One reason was my boyfriend, Russell. The other, more serious one, was that I had a million other ambitions and dreams. In class I had done quite well, especially in English, but I had been neither inspired nor encouraged to continue with a purely academic subject. Our P.E. classes were considered far more important; I was on the sports field every day unless I had a plaster cast on my leg and at one time I wanted very much to train as a dancer, even summoning up the courage to write to the choreographers Martha Graham and Merce Cunningham, who were then considered very avant-garde, for their advice. But that idea was soon replaced by a succession of other fantasies, some more realistic than others, but all sharing a high-flying, glamorous image. In my mind I became an opera singer, a veterinary surgeon, an actress and, after Vietnam started, a peace worker or social worker. There was only one thing I knew for sure – that I was never going to succumb to Polynesian paralysis and end up in a burger joint with a check hat and a frilly apron.

When we returned to Hawaii, I discovered that my best friend, who was supposedly looking after beefcake Russell, had instead run off with him. Trivial as teenage heartbreak may seem in retrospect, it is always devastating at the time. I was terribly shocked and hurt, vowed never to see either of them again and kept to my decision. I also decided, within a few days, to take up Kanebo's offer and return to Tokyo. It was a hasty decision and if circumstances had been different I might have bided my time and weighed up the opportunity against other routes out.

My family reacted to my decision to take up Kanebo's offer in very different ways: Suzon and Naomi were overcome by the idea of a glamorous adventure which would bring them presents, but my parents were very worried, knowing full well that I did not understand what I was taking on. By the time I got on the plane my excitement was mixed with a slight fear that I might have bitten off more than I could chew.

Initially, of course, I was swept along by the excitement and novelty value of my new life style. The work itself was very easy – although the hours were long. I was never expected to do anything for myself. Every day I would be picked up by car, taken to the studio to be made up, have my hair done and be dressed, then simply put in front of the camera like a doll to smile and look cute. It all seemed a bizarre parody of a dressing-up game. I even had regulation milk-and-cookie breaks during photo sessions and a private manager to chaperone me, make all my travel arrangements and generally mother me. But it was also tremendously exciting. In the first few weeks alone, they flew me first to Guam to model bikinis and then to the mountains, where I saw snow for the first time, to model ski clothes.

When I first arrived, I worried that Kanebo might suddenly discover all my bad points, like my teeth and lack of cleavage, and return me as faulty goods, but after they had spent several weeks telling me how perfect I was my fears melted away. The truth was that I fitted perfectly with their taste and aesthetic of beauty: an exotic little Hawaiian girl with long legs. Japan was then besotted with all things Western and, ideally, a model had to be a cross between all-American sweetness and Japanese innocence, which was exactly how I was promoted. Many of the other models in Japan at that time were also Amerasian. Known as *halfs*, they were the children of post-war GIs, both black and white, some of whom had grown up on the bases and were as American as popcorn, others of whom had grown up fatherless and could not speak a word of English, although they looked completely Western.

I was also buoyed along by the amount of money I was making. Apart from my contract money, I was paid for each assignment and so, instead of my hard-earned allowance of a few dollars, I suddenly had an envelope stuffed full of notes to spend every week. I went shopping as if there was no tomorrow, frittering it away like toy-town money on clothes and presents for my family and friends. I spent extraordinary sums on food. We had never eaten out much in Hawaii and now, like a child with its first box of chocolates, I wanted to try every kind of restaurant and flavour. There was so much I had never tasted before: cheese soufflé and crême caramel, smoked salmon and wine. I had never moved off the pizzas and my six-packs until then.

Glamour and food filled a void. Underneath the surface excitement, I was not really happy. It was not the ways of an alien culture, but the loneliness that got me down. At first I stayed with a friend of my parents, a very glamorous woman who looked like Ava Gardner – another childhood

A picture taken in Japan when I first started modelling. By this time they had already transformed me into a Japanese doll. It was a difficult period for me – I was trying so hard to please yet did not feel at ease with the image I was being made to project.

heroine – who had just married a well-known Samurai actor. She took me around all the smart clubs and restaurants and introduced me to the kingpins of the film and photographic world. But I missed my family desperately, nobody spoke English and I had no good friends of my own age. Despite the courtesy and gentleness of everyone I met through my work, the girls I worked with seemed suspicious of my friendliness and generosity with my new-found wealth and I think my success must inevitably have provoked jealousy that I was having such an easy time where others had to struggle. Perhaps I was too generous. Certainly, I had little judgment and often allowed myself to be taken for a ride.

After three months I decided to go home for a holiday. I remember arriving at Honolulu and spotting my family, who seemed open-mouthed in amazement at my sophistication. They rapidly disabused me. As my father succinctly put it, I looked as if I had been squeezed out of a sausage machine. The Japanese had never commented because they liked their dolls to be plump, but I had put on something like twenty pounds of weight, which on my bony frame looked a lot more. For the first time in my life, I went on a diet and after three miserable weeks of grilled fish and mineral water managed to shed my extra pounds.

Life in Japan improved on my return. Tina Lutz, now Tina Chow, who was then the top model in Japan, took me under her wing. Tina is also Japanese-American; the combination of Ohio gentility with Japanese taste and tact is fundamental to her style. Her parents, exactly like mine, had met during the American occupation, and she, too, had fallen accidentally into modelling. Her image, however, was subtly different with a little more emphasis on the Japanese side. Away from the camera, her sophistication is mixed with a mad zaniness and generosity which make her a wonderful friend. Kanebo managed to find me an apartment only a block away from her parents' house, which became my second home, and as my Japanese improved I gradually picked up other friends in the fashion and music business. I also found myself a boyfriend, a rock star called Shoken. Then he was tall, handsome and spoilt. Today he is a very successful actor.

Sudden saturation gives a very clear perspective on an alien culture, and with understanding I came to respect and appreciate Japanese attitudes. I kept the easy-going openness and lack of inhibition of my Hawaiian side, but it became smoothed down by the greater delicacy of Japanese ways. Quite often I would take the train and spend the weekend with my aunt and uncle, who owned a *tatami* inn in Hamamatsu. Uncle Chu, who had been a general in the Imperial Army until he had been blacklisted during the MacArthur period, was then one of the most famous *kingyo* goldfish breeders in Japan. Crossbred to have huge bubble heads, the fish are highly prized by the Japanese and change hands for thousands of dollars, but the correct markings can be picked out only by the skilled eye of the breeder from thousands of newly hatched eggs. Watching my uncle care for his fish was fascinating; they would come to his hands to be massaged. It was my first understanding of the aesthetics of perfection.

More gradually, I saw also that for the Japanese the single most important quality and fundamental ordering principle of life is courtesy: it permeates everything, producing a desire to please other people, an unwillingness to give offence in any way and the structured sense of orderliness that many Westerners find so hard to understand. Workers who are on strike, for example, do not actually stop work, which would be considered disruptive; they simply wear an armband to demonstrate their

Here I am in typical Hawaiian style: wearing nothing but a bikini with the ubiquitous flower behind my ear.

sympathies. Demonstrations are nearly always orderly, and any form of violence is deeply disturbing. I still sometimes find it difficult to be frank if I fear it might cause offence.

The Japanese attitude to art and the media is also very different. There is no dividing line between popular, or commercial, culture and fine art, and talent or beauty of any kind is revered with a public clamour that is quite unknown in the West. An artist like David Hockney is treated as a great celebrity and will be mobbed on the street and, in just the same way, fashion designers, photographers and models are appreciated as artists. Any category of artist can be honoured as a 'Living Treasure', one of the highest Japanese honours. At first I found it strange that literally hundreds of people would come to the signing sessions Kanebo arranged for me as their poster girl, but in the end I even became used to the idea that I had fan clubs and that people would approach me on the street.

Through the Japanese I learned to overcome my remaining inhibition about nakedness. On my bikini-modelling trip to Guam I was astonished to learn that a very young girl was doing some nude modelling, which I assumed must be for a men's magazine. I instinctively thought how shocked my father would be. It took me some time to realize that the Japanese have a category of public semi-nudity which does not exist in the West, representing a kind of clean and smiling innocence. In fact, in Japan it is illegal to show pubic hair in any form of publication. Neither sexual voyeurism nor shame are attached to the way it is photographed. All well-known personalities do nude posters which decorate the walls of nearly every home and are displayed in art galleries. This utterly different, open Japanese attitude made me look at my body in a new way and when I was nineteen I did a book of nudes for Shinoyama, Japan's most famous photographer at that time, with my brother and sisters. It was basically just the four of us having a good time on the beach without any swimming costumes on, but it would have been seen very differently in Europe.

I also picked up the Japanese open-mindedness about homosexuality and transvestism, which I had never encountered before. I had one great friend, a nightclub owner, whom I assumed to be a woman for weeks because he wore a kimono and, like all bar owners, was called Mama-san. Perhaps because I had a lot of fun with gays when I was so young, I have always felt completely at ease with homosexuality and greatly valued my gay friends. They are still my favourite dancing partners.

My first cover in Europe, wearing Kansai Yamamoto, photographed by Hiroshi.

I was learning a lot in some respects, but very little in others. Since I never thought of modelling as a long-term career, there seemed no reason to learn about my trade. Fortunately, I was jolted out of this by the photographer, Shinoyama. He saw me develop over the first year from a very shy, silent girl to a very talkative one. By the end of the year he was always regretfully saying, 'Mali' – this is how the Japanese pronounced my name – 'silence is golden'. One day he tactfully suggested, perhaps to try and keep me quiet, that I should try to learn about the processes and techniques involved in my work. I felt very ashamed and began to learn, simply by watching the other models, how to do my own make-up and hair, and how to walk down a catwalk. But it was impossible to pick up new approaches or see my work within any broader perspective because, although the Japanese adored fashion – and spent a lot on their clothes – nearly all Japanese designers were then simply aping European fashion and photographers aiming only to recreate shots from the latest issues of *Vogue* or *Elle*.

There were, of course, notable exceptions. Shinoyama was one of them, provocative and highly imaginative with his work. Fuji, Daiho and Tatsuki were with him. Among the designers, Issey Miyake, who was already a star in Japan, and Kansai Yamamoto, were producing wonderfully original clothes expressing an extraordinarily free spirit. Issey and Kansai were both great friends of mine. Issey is a highly intelligent, sensitive man, always searching for new experiences; I remember him telling me that he drank saki mixed with turtle's blood once a month to encourage his imagination and ideas to flow.

It was through Kansai, also a highly gifted designer and generous man, that I had my next great stroke of luck. He asked me to model his first collection in London in 1971, in a show inspired by kabuki theatre. Nothing like it had been done before. The show was to be performed on a stage rather than a catwalk, fully choreographed and stringently rehearsed. Our faces and bodies were to be hand-painted with tatoo-like motifs – and our eyebrows shaved off – in the traditional style. Kansai's concept was brilliant and it was perfectly suited to his designs, which were very avant-garde and highly theatrical. I had always loved kabuki, fascinated by both the element of ritual in the audience reaction – in sad parts, women will cry in unison – and the ceremony surrounding the performance itself, and was thrilled to be involved and to get a chance to go to London. We all sensed that this would be something special: by the time we reached London the word was out and the show was, deservedly, a sensation in both the fashion and performing arts worlds. The whole collection sold out and in the following year Kansai became costume director for David Bowie's world tour.

The show also launched me in London. Grace Coddington, the ex-model who as *Vogue*'s fashion editor discovered a lot of today's top models, and Barry Lategan, the photographer who had discovered Twiggy, asked me to do a photo session the next day. They must have thought me very tongue-tied. Yamamoto had given me strict instructions that I was on no account to spoil the mystique of the show by revealing offstage that I was American, so I obediently remained dumbstruck, opening my mouth as rarely as possible, and, when it seemed absolutely essential, speaking with a fake Japanese accent. The effect must have been very strange because people still comment on it.

The photo session turned out to be a baptism by fire to the tough world I would be taking on if I ever came to Europe. Maudie James, Kathy Damon and Moira Swan, who were then the most famous models in London and whose pictures I had seen in *Vogue*, were also in the shot. They all looked

quite perfect, and I felt ridiculous without my eyebrows. Kathy was really kind and did my make-up for me, but I sensed a tension and unfriendliness in the air that I had never encountered before as soon as I arrived in the dressing room.

I was amazed that nobody was talking and as the day wore on it became clear that I was meant to feel the resentment. At one point I tried to break the icy silence in the dressing room by asking casually what people in London did at night, to which one of them archly replied, with withering sarcasm, that everyone sat at home watching *Coronation Street*. 'What do you expect, darling?' She did not even lift her eyes as she buffed her nails. When we finally got in front of the camera, I had to stand as still as a statue with my hands on my hips. That finished me off and after only a few minutes I fainted.

Costumes from Kansai Yamamoto's kabuki show, photographed by Clive Arrowsmith for *Vogue*. Kansai made me parade the clothes up and down the King's Road – my embarrassment probably did not show under all the make-up.

THE
EYE OF
THE
CAMERA

Over the years the rather fragile exotic flower who first appeared in Europe grew into a worldly wise woman who could confront the illusion of the camera more honestly, with sex and strength, glamour and sophistication – but only after I had paid many times for her naiveté as she emerged from her chrysalis. The main problem was that my single greatest advantage as a model was also my greatest limitation: my *hapa-haole* looks always stood out, not only against almond-eyed oriental beauty, but also the blonde, blue-eyed type who pour into European model agencies. This made me unique, but, since my look tended to dominate any photograph, I could work less than other models in the early days.

The problem showed itself for the first time on my return to Japan after Yamamoto's show. I arrived back from all the excitement to be greeted by a lawsuit. One of the sponsors of the show turned out to be a textiles rival to Kanebo, who, justifiably annoyed, ended my contract after various negotiations. Fortunately, I could find plenty of other work, but it woke me up to the hazards of the market-place.

I stumbled again, and in a potentially more damaging way, a few months later after British *Vogue* had booked me, through Yamamoto, to do a cover shot in London. While I was there, another cover was arranged with *Harpers and Queen*, which I duly shot a week later. Although they were done by different photographers, the clothes and make-up were virtually identical. Thrilled by my luck, and blissfully unaware of the ludicrous impossibility that twin images could ever appear side-by-side on the news-stands, I returned to London a few months later to capitalize on such prestigious exposure, only to discover that I had lost the *Vogue* cover because it was going to be scooped by the press deadline. The mistake had not been mine, but I was going to pay the price.

It was thanks to those tough realities that doll-like Little Miss Cute began to grow up. During my early forays I was saved by the generosity of others. I had on my side the hand that can win any trick: the support of the right fashion editors and bookings from the right photographers. They gave me my first understanding of creative fashion photography. It was, above all, the difference between the approaches taken by Barry Lategan and Clive Arrowsmith, the two photographers with whom I first worked in Europe, that made me realize how much I had to learn.

Clive, with whom I did the lost *Vogue* cover, is without doubt one of the craziest people I have ever met. He was already very famous in Japan. My first encounter with him was more appropriate to a honky-tonk saloon in a frontier town than the sophisticated London fashion scene. I had just arrived at the *Vogue* offices and was standing, innocent and a little

awestruck, in the lift on the ground floor, when I noticed a gangly blond figure with hair below his shoulders, a sombrero worthy of Zapata and a low-slung belt with two guns loping towards me at great speed across the lobby. Looking nonchalant but feeling panicky, I pushed the lift button. Too late. He stuck a bronco boot between the doors, squeezed into the lift and proceeded to twirl his guns round his fingers like a rodeo star. After what felt like an eternity, during which he grinned knowingly and I shook in my shoes, we reached my floor. I shot out, only to be turned round by Grace Coddington so I could be introduced to the errant cowboy. This was the photographer with whom I would be working the next day.

That first session was hilarious, despite the theatrical solemnity of the poses: in fact, I think I spent more energy biting back laughter than holding the poses. I discovered then how Clive caught his extraordinary poses: through movement, caught in mid-air like suspended animation. He also loved any element of surprise and would do anything to provoke a reaction.

Barry Lategan, on the other hand, softly spoken, calm and gentle by nature, worked in Zen-like tranquillity to classical music and wanted long, static poses, only occasionally allowing me to sway very gently. He was a very caring, wonderfully loyal supporter, both as a photographer and as a friend.

In those first three months, I badly needed a friend. My hours at work were far more exciting than they had been in Japan, but when I went back to my hotel room at the end of the day, nothing awaited me. Some evenings I was very depressed. Although I felt at ease in London, I had neither the time nor the soul mates to take me beyond my disappointment that London was not the romantic city of my childhood dreams, with streets

lacquered by rain and fog cloaking mysterious night-time rendezvous. Instead it was a bland urban environment of long, empty evenings in unknown territory. I never glimpsed the heart of the city, and I missed the visual excitement of Tokyo, the delicacy of the Japanese spirit.

The pull between East and West set the pattern of my life for the next four years. Drawn to London, like a bee to a honey pot, by the stimulus and excitement of the work, yet never able to establish any personal life, I globetrotted back and forth following the routine of my three-month British work permits, wondering always whether I was about to say goodbye to Tokyo for the last time, but then finding it impossible to resist the lure of returning to friends and work there.

The European work-place was also frighteningly competitive. As I notched up my work permits, I began to get a perspective on my position within it. I had been very lucky in my timing for Europe: the playful clothes of the youthful sixties were followed by the more sophisticated fashions of the early seventies and models needed strong looks that would not be swamped by the clothes. When I first arrived there was a wild but feminine mood with colours used in an almost painterly way for a flowing, flamboyant effect. Make-up too had a subtle glamour which suited dark-eyed orientalism better than the looks of the traditional glossy cover-girl or the sixties waif. On the other hand, I did not suffer from the lack of height or other limitations of physique which held back the Mediterranean and Japanese girls. Barry Lategan, for example, covered my face with rainbow colours to create the effect of exotic blooms.

Nevertheless, it was difficult for me to make big money. The prestigious editorial work which I was getting – as distinct to commercial work, from

David Bailey and I did a series of advertisements for Olympus Cameras and for each ad I was photographed using the camera as a fashion accessory. The contact sheets (left) show me trying to find the right pose. I always look better in profile or with my face at an angle to the camera to disguise my lop-sided jaw. The markings are Bailey's and his final choice is shown here.

which I was excluded because I was too much of an exotic, often a derogatory euphemism for ethnic – was about the worst-paid in the business. A cover shot for *Vogue* or *Harpers and Queen*, for example, for whom I worked almost exclusively for several years, earned me the princely sum of £35 (and would earn little more today), while the more versatile advertising model who could plump out bras, wear diamond watches, scrub floors and still find the energy to serve up frozen food, or whose face was a more anonymous canvas on which a client or photographer could create the look they wanted, was then earning, at the very least, £200 a job and often a lot more. The same still holds true today, which is why it is so essential to be an all-rounder to make a good living as a model.

There were other restrictions, too, which I imposed upon myself. Firstly, I would not do commercial cosmetics shots, since nearly all the large companies used animals for testing. I lost a lot of work like that, but I believe strongly that there are more humane – and more scientific – alternatives to vivisection and testing on animals. Secondly, I would not – and still will not – work with furs, as I do not believe in the deliberate killing of animals for adornment. Of course, if I had said that I objected on moral grounds, I would have been thrown out of every studio in town, so I simply used to say I was allergic to it. It is a small stand to take not to model beauty or fashion that brings unnecessary cruelty, but in my view a necessary one to preserve self-respect. As a result, my bank statements were often distressing columns of red figures. I would take a quick peep at the figure at the bottom, and then try to forget it as I sleuthed down the cheapest possible flight to Tokyo.

But every pound sterling I lost was worth its weight in gold. I was immeasurably lucky to work with fashion at its very best, in terms of both its design and its depiction. The scope offered by editorial work of that kind stimulates very creative and demanding photography. I had to teach myself and I tripped up many times on the way, but I slowly began to see my role as that of an actress who should create and control the element of illusion – to learn to choose the roles I could play well, to master the techniques of performing for a lens and to acquire a sense of the market-place in which my image was sold.

I would dutifully do my homework. A model never gets the chance to see the photographer's contact sheets, but I would scrutinize the finished shots in magazines to see how my imperfections had been highlighted by the lens and how I could compensate for them through pose, angle of the head, make-up or hair. Equally, I studied marketing in order to understand how different clients would want their clothes presented. After all, in the end I was selling a product – or, as Diana Vreeland would say, in her inimitable way, we were there to sell frocks.

Soon I also made it part of my homework to scan all the fashion magazines at my end of the market to pick up new ideas for poses, comparing the way flat shoes and high heels or the lengths of a hemline affected the way I looked, and perfecting the crucial finishing touches, like the positioning of hands, in front of a mirror.

Posing was just starting to become far more complex at the time I arrived in Europe because as fashions became less extreme, the impact of a photograph depended far more on dynamic poses suggesting movement, drama or mood to command the readers' attention. Contrary to many people's expectations, static poses are as difficult as movement shots, especially when they are contrived, as they were in the early seventies. The

Modelling clothes by Gianni Versace designed around a Polynesian theme. The Italian photographer, Gianpaulo Barbieri, always looks for pure glamour – he is the only photographer I know who allows his models to work with a full length mirror.

art, I learned, was to bear in mind the separate elements of a good performance – artifice, awareness of the camera and a self-critical eye for detail – and still manage to keep a natural expression. Movement shots, on the other hand, require much greater concentration on the clothes, since the way they fall is determined by the motion of the body, not the pins of the stylist. Often I repeat a simple movement, like an arch of the back, shake of the head or bounce to the music, again and again, so the photographer can catch exactly the right moment where everything pulls together.

As I discovered by trial and error what made me look good or bad in photographs, I could hand that knowledge back to the photographer. After a while I knew exactly which one of a dozen facial expressions or looks to use for a shot without being told, and could call them up at will as easily as pressing a button. I also began to regard much more of what went on in the dressing room as my area of responsibility. However uncivilized the hour of the day and however strong the urge to lie back and doze, I would always leave in my contact lenses and watch the make-up artist and hairdresser like a hawk to check that I was not going to end up looking like a dog's dinner – or with all the points the fashion editor had paid for carefully disguised.

My experience working for *Vogue* and *Harpers and Queen*, particularly with Barry Lategan, was, quite literally, the passport that took me to the top. Through Barry, I went to collections fortnight in Rome on my second visit to England and then on to Milan and Paris, Germany and New York.

My exoticism gave me a flying start on the Continent, especially in Italy, where the taste in models has always been far more adventurous and extravagant than that of either London or Paris, and I landed commissions for Italian and French *Vogue*, working with wonderful photographers like Barbieri in Milan and Jean Loup Sieff and Jean Jacques Bugat in Paris. Arthur Elgort, who was then just starting out, was also working in France at that time. His more informal style, which did so much to change the way fashion was photographed in America, was already very different from those of the classic European untouchables and anticipated the energetic exuberance that dominated American fashion photography by the end of the decade.

Sessions in Milan were much crazier than those in London and Paris, with plenty of Latin temperament and extravagance in evidence. But collections fortnight in Rome beats all-comers for atmosphere, hilarity and bizarre spectacle. The sessions, which take place in a large studio complex resembling twentieth-century catacombs and start only in the early evening after the clothes have been delivered from the shows, are an extraordinary slice of *la dolce vita*. The fashion editors have chosen the clothes at the shows and the dresses move around from studio to studio in strict order of seniority, beginning with the Americans – *Vogue, Harpers Bazaar* and *Women's Wear Daily* – followed by French and Italian *Vogue*, then *Elle*. As the cool of the day turns to night, the photographers and their teams make their entrances. Editors stand knotted in animated argument, discussing personal favourites among the dresses that stole the shows. Models, hairdressers and aristocratic Romans drape themselves elegantly around tables heaped with food and drink. Then everyone retreats behind closed doors to shoot in honour-bound secrecy, emerging occasionally to watch the Fellini-esque world go by in the corridors. The photography itself is often bizarre, in part because the classic quality of couture clothes relies on the way it is shown to make it interesting. Slowly, hard-core craziness sets in. I remember many bizarre scenarios on these long journeys through the night: a worried photographer passing off caffeine tablets wrapped in foil as speed for a flagging model – a shocking sight to me then – and a would-be starlet wandering around naked with an extraordinary series of synthetic curves on display. She wore her silicone with pride. I cannot imagine why.

That same year – 1972 – I made a lengthy expedition to New York, only to discover that I was very definitely in the wrong place at the wrong time. And by the wrong time, I mean almost ten years too early. All they wanted on that side of the Atlantic were clean-living slices of home-grown cheesecake with turned up noses, blue eyes and freckles, who looked good frolicking in a haystack in jeans and pigtails. Not quite my style. 'European' was, if not exactly a term of abuse, applied indiscriminately to anything that looked different or exciting: this whole approach to fashion seemed like a travesty when compared to the exuberance of someone like Issey Miyake, who was, even then, using clothes to show people how to feel free. St Laurent, too, was then considered European – and, therefore, pretty much out for the count. I was even worse; I was distinctly foreign.

I had been invited to go to New York by the late Wilhelmina, one of the top agents and an ex-model herself, on the strength of my work for *Vogue*. I stayed for six months, got plenty of bookings and, because the American scene has always meant big bucks, was set to earn far better money than I ever could in the cottage industry of seventies London. But I could not crack through the barrier of taste to the prestige jobs that would make it worth my while to stick around. Incredible as it may sound, the racial conservatism in American modelling remained such that American *Vogue* did not get its first black cover-girl, Beverley Johnson, until 1974 – eleven years after the 1964 Civil Rights Act and two years after my visit. Now it is illegal for a shot with four or more models not to have a token black or exotic, but advertisers and fashion magazines still do not give them the space justified by the millions of consumers who would be more likely to buy clothes and cosmetics if they saw ethnic women modelling them. I never accept jobs where I feel I am being used as a forced gesture.

I was not sad to leave New York. As a city I found it alien. The speed, the ceaseless noise and the seediness of the narrow, grid-like streets cutting across the concrete jungle of towering blocks overpowered me with a stifling sense of threat. That sense of menace dogged me and I eventually left after one of my greatest friends, a Japanese art student who had been working for the artist Jasper Johns, was murdered over the Christmas holiday. I was in Hawaii at the time and intending to return, but I simply abandoned my belongings. Some places are not worth the struggle.

I found New York fashion photography equally alien. Where in Europe, the imagination and the originality of the photographer's conception set the pace, here, it seemed, only organization and efficiency seemed to count, and the model seemed to matter more than the photographer. A famous face made the shot. The only photographers with whom I would have loved to work, Richard Avedon and Irving Penn, who had been photographing Paris glamour since Dior's New Look, were then way out of reach. 'Just keep on schedule, baby, and move on to the next session', as one make-up artist advised me without irony. I could not enjoy such a clock-and-dollar approach after the spontaneity of open-ended European sessions, which for all their late morning starts and long delays while the lighting was changed or the set repainted in the middle of a shot, produced far better photographs. It is a good indicator that American models have always come to Europe to get creative and original tear-sheets for their portfolios. In some respects I suppose I did become a lot more professional in my attitudes: on my very first day Wilhelmina gave me an accounts book to note my expenses for tax purposes, and I learned then that a nine o'clock start meant exactly that by American – if not Hawaiian – time. In my heart, though, I knew these were not the qualities of a really good model, but the accoutrements of the professional.

My apparently glamorous jet-setting life meant a distinctly impoverished personal life. Shortly after my first long trip to London I split with my Japanese boyfriend and no lasting relationship replaced it for four years. There was space only for ships that passed in the night. Everything was contingent upon work and I worked from sun-up till sun-down: if my agent called me at nine a.m. with a job for eleven, I would be there – and if that meant being at the airport ready to go to Timbuktu or the North Pole, I would be packed and waiting at the check-in desk. As a result, my only friends for years were from work, because I never had time to do anything other than eat, sleep and breathe fashion. Some were other models, like Angelica Huston and Pat Cleveland, who were often passing through town; I kept in touch with Tina Lutz, too, who had by now married the restaurateur Michael Chow. Others were designers, like Zandra Rhodes, who took me under her wing just as Tina had done in Japan, or people I had met through fashion journalism, like Barney Wan and Grace Coddington. People were always passing or disappearing, so it was difficult to strike up lasting, close relationships. I did not want a wild social life, but it would have been nice to be an irresponsible young girl, burning the candle low and sleeping late the next morning, instead of which I was always in the make-up chair by breakfast time.

Photographers did not figure so much until I met Bailey. Arthur Elgort, who always kept open house for models after he had moved back to the States, was an exception, as was Barry Lategan. He was my closest friend and I would write him long letters from Japan. Essentially, photographers are a breed of loners, and, as a model, there is never time to get to know them during a session. The pace of the profession is very fast, too; many sink without trace after a few years. Others choose to move on. The best fashion photographs are taken not by fashion photographers – a media invention of the sixties – but photographers who happen to be doing fashion and who often inhabit very different worlds.

There was a similar prosaic reality behind the glossy, daydream quality of the photographs. There is a well-known modelling story about a famous French photographer that sums up this reality. A model had to have silver powder blown in her eyes for a special effect. She must have known that for days she would suffer from red, swollen eyes and be unable to work, but she must also have known there would be magic in the photograph. She did not refuse although she had the right to do so, and I wonder if I would have done the same.

Another, more hilarious, misconception in the mind of the reader is that of constant sexual electricity – static flying between the model and the photographer. People are always asking whether fashion photographers are sex machines with Nikons, perhaps because of their image in the sixties, or because there is an idea that modelling must involve seduction since somewhere along the line women are taking off their clothes. I suppose there must be a few photographers whose main preoccupation is to go to bed with the model, but most of the ones I know are hard-working professionals well past sowing their wild oats who are far too concerned

Models very rarely get to know photographers well but in this case I was lucky. Here I am with Helmut Newton, a good friend and a great photographer.

with the complexities of photography to be thinking sexually about the model. Male models are also often lumbered with the playboy image. Again, nothing could be further from the truth: in the old days they were more likely to ask to borrow my mascara than to try for a kiss. Today, of course, they have become huge stars, but they are still equally detached and far less typecast. Some are resting brain surgeons, others ex-gasolene attendants. In either case, they are laughing all the way to the bank.

If the shot disallows either of these assumptions, people like to assume the model is fantasizing. Equally untrue. I perform, not to the eye of the man behind the camera, but to the lens, and what looks right for a photograph would never work in the eye of the beholder. An embrace for the camera is an arrangement of the arms; a kiss or a pout, a contrived arrangement of the lips. Looking sexy is never the product of passion and I am never feeling the emotion apparently captured in my eyes. Clark Gable did it by thinking about a raw steak and I do it by slightly closing my eyes and parting my mouth. As for the mind, I am always thinking about the lighting or the tilt of my jawbone, or – in a distracted moment – the dry cleaning and the fish for supper. The moment the roll of film is finished, I simply stretch like anyone leaving their desk at the end of the day and hurry off to get changed. The glamour is only ever in the finished photograph. The rest is a combination of hard work, foolhardiness, boredom and laughter – the last you have to find youself along the way.

So much was a question of that old Hollywood adage, 'Hurry up and wait'. For every minute in front of the camera there were hours spent marking time with a book or a cup of tea and an endless stream of dressing-room gossip, sometimes funny but often bitchy, about who had looked

good and who had looked awful, how much people were earning, and whose hair was falling out in clumps or who had ears like an African elephant. Quite often I would be ready for the shot by ten after an eight o'clock start, but would still be sitting around at noon as the photographer's assistant was unrolling the backdrop of white paper and putting the spotlights in position.

Finally the music would start to kill the dead atmosphere of the studio and I would move on to the paper. Then there was more waiting, this time under sweltering bright lights while a dress that was one size too large or small was fixed up with pins, or the pose altered to give exactly the right folds in a dress. Every part of a model's appearance is tweaked into position at the last moment. Quite often the assistant would be crouching just off the camera pulling the clothes into the clean, taut lines the photographer wanted. Occasionally, sessions even had to be artificially dragged out by the photographer so that the client did not feel cheated. Worst of all were the shots of heavy winter coats done in an airless studio on a boiling summer's day, with banks of film lights only feet away and the make-up artist rushing forward every few seconds to blot the shiny perspiration with more powder. I have always had a famous star turn: fainting. First my limbs would tingle, then they would become numb and, finally, after eight or ten minutes in a pose, I would keel over and land in a heap on the floor. The problem became so bad that I went to a doctor in the hope of finding a miracle cure, but since the cause was mundane poor circulation, fidgeting was the only remedy. That produced nearly as many complaints as a faint. Such is the reality behind the illusion of effortless beauty.

Occasionally, I was foolhardy. Once I dangled over the rooftops of Rome

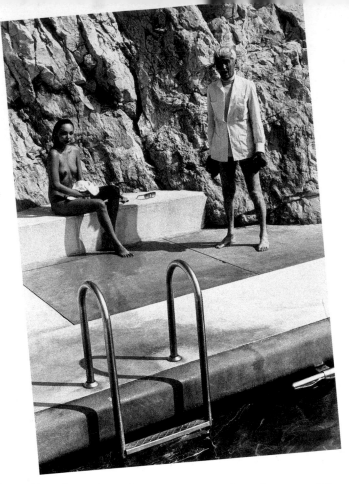

while Gina Lollobrigida took a series of pictures at receding distances. The French fashion editor was furious with me, but I liked the idea. Twice, I abandoned my better judgment and agreed to work with animals. On both occasions it was grotesque. The first time, working with Albert Watson in New York, I had to hold the hand of a chimp; it felt uncannily human, but the palm was far sweatier and it clasped me with unexpected power. The second time, in Germany, was worse. I should have backed out as soon as the poor animal arrived. It was supposed to be a baby leopard, but turned out to be the size of a Great Dane and arrived very heavily sedated, carried in by the trainer, whose lower arms were ripped from elbow to wrist by scar tissue. The art director expected me to hold it; I flatly refused. We compromised. I would lie down and hold up its head. I managed to get into the pose, but I began to feel nauseous with mingled disgust and terror and allowed my arms to slacken after only five shots. The leopard's head slumped sickeningly like that of a dead animal. It was too much and I walked out.

The occupational hazards of the studio are nothing, however, in comparison with those of the location. They usually start with a dawn call to catch the sun while it is still low and end in a sand dune or market, with sand blowing in your eyes or a crowd watching you touch up your eye make-up. One of the worst was a rice paddy full of stagnant water and buffalo dung in Bali. Afterwards I had to clean my itching feet and calves in the only disinfectant available – a bottle of duty-free whisky. The hotels were often worse than the poses. I remember a hole-in-the-ground lavatory next to a sink full of squirming larvae in Indonesia and another black moment in a Sri Lankan hotel room spotted by countless crimson patches marking the previous guests' revenge on the lethal resident mosquitoes. When I asked at the hotel desk for a net without gaping holes they simply laughed in my face.

The grand old man of French photography, Jacques Henri Lartigue, whom I think of more as a friend with a terrific sense of humour. Bailey once nicknamed Lartigue the Proust of photography because of his ability to record the flavour of the times by capturing the decisive moment. Jacques always makes me feel beautiful. He took this photograph (right) in the pool at the Hotel du Cap, Antibes.

At certain points – not always the black moments – I would look back and realize how far I had travelled since my Japanese days as a doll in a glorified dressing-up game. The elementary understanding of photography I had gleaned from my sessions with Clive Arrowsmith and Barry Lategan was now on much surer footing. An innate sense of graceful movement is priceless for a model and if she has the right alchemy in front of the camera, not even a dud hairstyle can stop the magic. But her, or his, potential cannot be realized without certain techniques of performance which only develop slowly over years of assimilation. It was through experience, and trial and error, that I came to understand the reasons for the photographer's instructions – for example, what was wanted when I was asked for a stronger shape. I also developed a much greater sympathy with the working styles of individual photographers. Perhaps the most important difference is the involvement and speed with which they work. At one end of the spectrum would be Bruce Weber, the American star of the eighties, who is often so involved with the people he works with that they move into his house in Connecticut – along with their friends, relations and pets – and at the other are those, like Bailey, who believe you should have the picture in the first ten shots. Today there are few who still use four or five rolls of film on the same dress in the same pose though Guy Bourdin, the French photographer, is legendarily said to take up to three days to get a shot right and to be so involved with the photograph that he forgets the model. Then, more technically, I learned how to adjust my performance for particular pieces of equipment: that while there is a margin for movement and a helpful rhythm to working with a 35mm camera with a motor drive, for example, there can be no errors with an old-fashioned plate camera occasionally used by a very experienced photographer. The exposure time is so much longer and the film very expensive. I came instinctively to look for the main source lights so I could ensure that I angled my face properly with the light falling directly over the nose.

One of the most valuable gifts a model can have is the sympathy to surrender her individuality to the photographer's vision. That varies a great deal, in both obvious and subtle ways. Barry Lategan portrayed me with tenderness and discreet eroticism as an oriental flower. Lartigue caught the same fleeting sense of romance he had used to capture the exquisite Parisian beauties of the twenties; his crystal-clear eyes always twinkled with a teasing flirtatiousness. Barbieri portrayed all his models with an untouchable sense of glamour, almost as a fantasy projection of himself. Clive Arrowsmith, on the other hand, never lost his inimitable sense of humour and playful movement; he would catch me falling out of a funny pose or make me stick my finger up my nose and still somehow make me look glamorous. Helmut Newton, who usually portrays his models as strong and aggressive, never seemed to take me very seriously at all – I was always giggling in his pictures.

Women, on the other hand, look for more honesty and less of a painted expression, and I think they have a knack of getting it. They tend to make me nervous because I find it difficult to present them with a simple image of beauty. Of the women fashion photographers, I have worked only with Sarah Moon, but I admire very much the work of other women. Helmut Newton's wife, June, for example, a marvellous portrait photographer who works under the name Alice Springs, has a rare ability to win the sympathy of all her sitters. She never imposes her own ego on the portrait. Annie Liebovitz, who has taken a few private snaps of me, has a quite different,

Sadly I only met Cecil Beaton once, a few months before he died. He never took my photograph, which I would have greatly valued. I do, however, have several of his prints which I bought at auctions.

slightly wild enthusiasm which is very infectious. Parts of my personality always came through in photographs. Other layers, more difficult to perceive at first glance, were often missed in the early days.

It was only with Bailey that those came to the surface. He made me think about the way I was being depicted and whether or not I really liked it. That finally brought out the woman I wanted to be rather than the woman that other people thought I was: I stopped surrendering myself to the camera and gave my self instead. Now, ten years later, the enigmatic but slightly aggressive and self-conscious style he pulled out is the only way I like to be photographed.

It may seem strange that it took so long for our paths to cross in the small world of London fashion, but I had such a stylized image that a fashion editor would have needed X-ray eyes to predict the chemistry. We could have saved four years if Bailey had not missed my kabuki debut to skip off to Mick and Bianca Jagger's wedding, but I probably would not have spotted him in the crowd. He certainly would not have been able to see me under the make-up. The delay was definitely a good thing. Even when I knew exactly what I was doing in front of the camera four years later, I found the prospect of working with Bailey pretty daunting.

When Beatrix Miller, editor-in-chief of British *Vogue*, announced to me at the Paris collections that she wanted me to go and see him about a possible *Vogue* booking my reaction was one of nervous anticipation as much as excitement. The nerves were justifiable. I knew exactly what was at stake for me professionally. For over ten years, since Bailey had become the *enfant terrible* of photography with his portraits of swinging London and his fashion shots with Jean Shrimpton, it had been considered the highest

accolade for a model to be one of Bailey's Girls: he liked to use very few models and to build up a working rapport with them over a long period of time. This was a rare opportunity. I knew, also, that because he always had a say on the model used for a shot, the booking depended entirely on what he thought of me.

My nerves sprung equally from the mystique and endless gossip that seemed to gather around Bailey's name. He had been famous for as long as I could remember; while I was still doing my bust exercises in the kitchen, he and Catherine Deneuve had been billed as the most beautiful couple in the world. I could also remember a visit he had made to Hawaii with Penelope Tree because a schoolfriend had pointed out her photograph in the local press, commenting on our resemblance. At the time I was not too flattered by the comparison. I think that my American tastes rather blinded me to the compliment.

Once inside the blasé, fickle world of fashion Bailey's mystique became even greater. He had a terrible and quite unfounded reputation for rudeness and temperamental behaviour. This, I later discovered, was in part due to his involvement in his work. Quite rightly, I think, he throws any girl who yawns with boredom out of the studio on the grounds that she could at least show a bit of interest if everyone else is working their arse off to make her look good. The reputation was also based on the bare-faced lies told by girls who wanted to boost their dressing-room status by claiming they had worked with him and on awestruck models' stupidity. Bailey told me once of a very famous American model who he asked to hold a perfect pose and who did not realize he had gone to lunch. When he returned, two hours later, he found that she had remained, frozen rigid, in exactly the same position.

The other side of the coin, Bailey's reputation as a rakish womanizer who had turned every sixties fashion editor's knees to jelly was somewhat closer to the truth. When we met, the precise topic of Bailey gossip was the break-up of his seven-year relationship with Penelope Tree – perfect dressing-room scandal, of course, since it involved a model as well. His wild days, however, had been his youth. One evening at La Coupole, the legendary Parisian restaurant, he bet Roman Polanski the cost of the meal that he could seduce one of the women in the restaurant before the bill arrived. He picked out a well-known fashion editor among the diners, she proved willing to be hauled off to his Rolls Royce – and the consequence was that Polanski paid the bill. Another evening, when he was sitting in Mr Chow with David Putnam and his agent, his eye failed him badly. Urged on by them, he went over to the table of a woman with beautiful legs who had been flirting with him across the restaurant. She mysteriously knew his name, but he could not even recognize her, let alone remember her as a brief encounter. She eventually had to tell him that they had not only known each other intimately, but had also been down the aisle together.

Bailey and I met at the *Vogue* offices as planned. He was sitting on the floor, absorbed in a magazine layout, with a cigarette hanging out of his mouth. He was pleasant, mentioning that he had heard of me because he knew who all the good models were. I found him very attractive physically – I always had gone for the dark, intense Heathcliffe type – and I thought I also felt a strange, mutual spark of recognition, an instinctive knowledge that we could learn a great deal from one another. But he had been very non-committal and offhand and I left feeling unsure whether I would even get the job. The following week my agent confirmed the booking.

A perceptive woman's portrait, and one of my personal favourites, by Alice Springs.

THE BAILEY DECADE

I was so jittery that I hardly slept a wink the night before the first day of the sitting and, to make matters worse, when I got to the studio the following morning with a hole in my stomach eaten by nerves, I found myself confronted with the task of doing my own face because the make-up artist, Barbara Daly, had fallen sick. I ploughed ahead hoping for the best, but knowing also that Bailey had a very perfectionist and critical eye. Fortunately, he seemed happy with what I had managed to do. Actually, I think he was rather impressed.

The chemistry in the camera was instant. Bailey communicated to me his passion for the camera and I respected rather than resented his desire for control and did not interfere with his work. For both of us, the model and photographer had their own jobs to do. Equally, I was good at understanding and following his instructions; I could interpret his sign language so well that there was no need for speech other than the occasional unforced exclamation or word of encouragement.

We hardly exchanged a word for the first two days – there simply was not time. Then, on the third day, when the pace began to let up, we began chatting, especially about my background. It turned out Bailey had originally taken me to be Brazilian. His intense gaze made me feel nervous and I found it hard to look him in the eye, but I could sense that he liked me and at the end of the session he gave me a lift home. I felt very tongue-tied: I think I managed to comment that I thought it would snow the next day. As I went through the door I remember feeling slightly heady with elation, and I knew it was more than my tiredness or relief that it had gone so well.

Before I had much time to reflect on my own feelings, Bailey and I were seeing each other through work almost every day. The atmosphere of the studio in his house was quite different to that of Barry's: it was always a madhouse, with a lot of noise and rock music blaring in the background. Bailey's approach was entirely different too. He preferred to find variety through photography rather than the novelty of fashion. Once he knew my face, he knew exactly how he wanted to light it, and I learned never to angle my head too low for him. He was also meticulous about poses, from the positioning of a little finger to a stray wisp of hair; nothing escaped his beady eyes. Only if he became stuck would he ask me to help him out or show him what I could do within the frame.

On the other hand, he was constantly experimenting with lighting and lenses, backdrops and cameras, new ideas and themes to highlight the clothes. One year, for Yves St Laurent's collection designed in homage to Picasso, he drew a backdrop of enormous plastic linear figures reminiscent of Picasso's style and shot the clothes against them. With each model came new inspiration, new ideas and even new techniques. Sometimes I was spellbound by the photography to the detriment of the pose. The first time we worked with a plate camera, a famous occasion that I have never been allowed to forget, I was so mesmerized that when Bailey carelessly commented that I should see how sensational the shot looked in the viewfinder, I was there in a flash, completely forgetting that the picture had walked away with me.

Far more than this, though, it was extraordinarily exhilarating to work with someone who encouraged and dared me to give more and more of myself, who wanted mystery rather than a painted face and allowed me to hold nothing back as a model. Despite Bailey's directorial – some say dictatorial – approach, I quickly realized that his apparent will for complete control is deceptive. Our ideas of femininity require that the fashion model must surrender herself to the implacable eye of the camera in order to be portrayed as a glamorous object, vulnerable but unavailable. But the very essence of Bailey's style is his refusal to allow his models to be simply clothes-hangers or his pictures moments of fashion. He photographs women wearing clothes. In order to do that, he surrenders the mood and style of the picture to the personality of the model. Where he is directorial is in his judgment of how best to make that work in the eye of the camera.

It is because Bailey makes the personality of the model his starting point that he has working habits often attributed to eccentricity or arrogance: his preference for working with a few hand-picked girls with whom he feels he can build up a mutual rapport, his selection of models with personality rather than classical beauty and his insistence that his models like the self-image the camera is recording so that they will not hold back from the camera. If there was any doubt in my mind about the way I looked, he simply would not continue, and I was not getting special treatment – the same holds true for all his models. Many was the time I slipped the dress off my shoulder, rather than wear it formally as the fashion editor had planned. After being at the whim of fashion editors' tastes, that was an enormous breath of fresh air. Bailey is also very easy-going about when he starts shooting – never until mid-morning, even if everything had been set up well before. Or, as he tells clock-watching art directors with a roguish glint in his eye, you never can tell what a girl has been up to the night before. She has to have time to unwind.

As a model, I think Bailey's approach pays dividends. It is a completely logical approach to the psychology of selling clothes. Fashion, after all, is about the people who are wearing it, and the first thing a woman looks at in a magazine is the model's face. If the reader likes the face, she is far more likely to look at the dress. And the face will only look good if the model gives the personality behind it to the camera. Any model knows the difference between being photographed by a mediocre fashion photographer and a top one. Tania Mallet, the top sixties model, once said that being photographed by Avedon was like 'having your soul sucked out through your eye sockets'.

It took me a long time to recognize the warning signs that I was falling for Bailey. We rarely spoke during sessions and I nearly always took off for home immediately afterwards. Perhaps I had been desensitized by the chemistry in the camera, or perhaps he was simply the first man I fell in love with. The signs finally came on an airplane between Paris and London. I was returning from a modelling job in Paris, and he was on his way back from a party in Mexico, looking very scruffy in a grubby pair of jeans and an old

The Brazil shoot: my first session with Bailey. The shot was set against a back-projection of tropical Brazil that he had taken on a recent trip there. When these pictures came out, everyone wanted to know who the new Brazilian model was.

The bed shoot: my second session with Bailey. This time the shot was set against his bedroom. Within a few months the bed had become mine, too, and we shared it for over a decade.

leather jacket. I had spotted him in the airport lounge, lurking restlessly in the shadow of Patrick Lichfield, who was sporting an outsized Stetson and looking very elegant by contrast with Bailey. I kept my distance. Then I discovered, to my surprise, that Bailey had the seat next to mine on the plane. I looked down and saw on his feet a pair of fatally beautiful shoes, a pair of co-respondent black-and-white Fred Astaires. They were his party shoes, but he had not bothered to change them. It said so much about Bailey. When I confessed to him a long time later that I blamed everything on those shoes, he admitted that he had raced Lichfield down the aisle of the plane to grab the seat next to me. It was a good thing he won.

Several more weeks passed before Bailey found the courage to make a move. Late one night, at the end of a photo session, he finally asked me if I would like to go out with him one evening. I was somewhat taken aback. The evening started romantically. Bailey came to pick me up at the flat and we dutifully sat on opposite sides of the room like nervous teenagers on a first date. Then, however, it turned out that he had arranged for us to go out *à quatre*, with Beatrix Miller and Barney Wan, the art director of *Vogue*, not, as I had imagined, *à deux*, with just a little background music for company. Typical Bailey.

For a while the affair continued in that vein, very lightly, and almost as a natural extension of our working day. He had a great knack of making me feel good about myself. My individuality, which was simply a refusal to live

up to other people's standards, apparently made me special. It was also a rare treat to find a soul mate who inhabited the same world as me and had a sense of humour about it. We would have long bantering sessions at the end of the day, taking the mickey out of the fashion industry. Nobody was spared: I was often being told I should have stayed up in the coconut trees.

Yet for the first time in my life, I was made to feel beautiful. Bailey made me aware of my sexuality. He told me I had the most beautiful body he had ever seen. That was extraordinary to me. As Bailey began to ask me out very persistently, I began to realize he had fallen for me. We still had a lot of fun, but now I felt nervous. Many of my best friends kept warning me that I would simply become another name on the list, and it was hard to dismiss his reputation and their well-meaning advice. I knew another girl had moved in with him since Penelope Tree had left and I imagined myself being slotted into some kind of rota system. I was also awestruck by Bailey himself. That may sound laughable, but he was looked on by most of the people with whom I worked as some kind of hero and I was still so unsure of myself with only a couple of teenage romances behind me.

But as Bailey began to relax with me, I could not help my feelings deepening. I quickly discovered that the public image was a poor caricature. His qualities are not immediately apparent, but as soon as he is at ease, his gentleness and softer side begin to slip out despite himself; it is no accident that children gravitate towards him even though he claims to have no interest in them. Yet with my own childish lack of confidence, I did not so much come to love Bailey, as to hero-worship him. Everything he said sounded right. He filled me with admiration and he made me feel completely safe.

By now we were seeing each other every evening, but I would only go to

his house for work and adamantly refused to stay the night. This was my first grown-up affair – my first serious relationship since coming to Europe – and I was worried that guilt would sour the perfection. Since we wanted to relax together in the evenings without waking up one day to find Fleet Street standing on the doorstep, I moved in with Grace Coddington and the photographer Willie Christie, who were then husband and wife and had both known Bailey for some years. Their affection for him increased my trust in him, and my confidence in my own sense of judgment. But I began to feel increasingly awkward about anybody at all knowing that Bailey was coming up to my room and, looking for complete privacy and anonymity for my emotions, I moved out to the Portobello Hotel. Work continued to extend the amount of time we spent together. We were not simply a good team, we also had our timing right, and although we did not try to formulate or develop a set image, a look evolved from picture to picture which perfectly suited the strong, deliberately sexy fashions of the mid-seventies. His main personality model since Penelope Tree, who had been perfect for the extremism of the hippy sixties, had been Angelica Huston – to my mind one of the real beauties of the seventies with a very unconventional glamour – but she had just taken off for the States because she had started going with Jack Nicholson. I fitted the empty space perfectly. It was exactly the right moment for an exotic who could look Brazilian one day and oriental the next, who was mysteriously unsmiling, sleek and untouchable, but with a suggestion of hidden tenderness. Bailey hated the coloured paints most photographers had used on me and he darkened my eyes in a much more sultry, womanly way. The fashion editors loved it.

It felt increasingly unnatural to live apart. The unwanted girl had by now moved out, but I still worried that the bed would feel warm. Only after the bliss of four whole days and nights together on our first working trip abroad, in Italy, did I finally move in. For me it was an enormous step. I spent my first week overwhelmed by embarrassment, convinced that Bailey's friends would take me for a fly-by-night playmate, and that his staff might think of me as some shameless hussy who had washed up off the streets. I cared desperately that our relationship should not be misinterpreted. The first evening I shut myself in the bedroom when an unsuspecting Italian friend of Bailey's appeared, and I absolutely refused to come out. Worse still, I was so terrified of being seen to play the presumptuous mistress of the house that the following day I sat in the bathroom, the only room I knew apart from the bedroom, until Bailey came home from work late in the afternoon.

The household was pretty extraordinary. Behind the scruffy blue facade were six floors of late sixties settings, including the obligatory Black Room and the Purple Room, which was a spare bedroom complete with hand-painted pink minarets. Every wall and surface was spilling over with photographs, paintings, books and artefacts in a quirky jumble that had little regard for culture or period, but a marvellous eye for image and form. Bailey shared it all with sixty parrots, several dogs, passing friends and Cezar, who looked after the house. Cezar, in particular, could not have been more welcoming, and I began to realize that I was not considered as an outsider. Gradually, I moved in my possessions and cats. I brought some of my own taste to the house, covering the Black Room with splashes of colour, abolishing the pink minarets from the Purple Room and filling the whole house with more light.

Bailey and I spent many evenings together in favourite restaurants. The press, of course, took full advantage of this and I soon got to know the first names of most of the photographers waiting to catch a shot.

The hidden Bailey, taken by me in Mexico.

After so many years alone, it was an extraordinary pleasure to come to rest at last, and to share small everyday pleasures with somebody I loved. Our relationship was very playful. Bailey had the worst household habits in the world: when we were watching television he was always idly picnicking and slinging the apple cores and empty coke tins over his shoulder. I knew it was not worth trying to change him. Instead, I simply refused to clear up after him unless I felt emergency measures were necessary. Quite often I would throw his smelly shoes and socks out of the bedroom window when we went to bed. He would never go down for the socks, but always for the shoes. Bailey had his own means of revenge. He often suggested I should get to know the Hoover better and he always sulked if I went out in flat shoes because he claimed they made me look like Minnie Mouse. I refused to pick up the hints.

I found no problem surrendering my independence because we already knew each other's quirks so well. I began slowly to change, not so much physically as mentally. The fact that Bailey believed in me so much made an extraordinary difference to my self-esteem; he gave me a wonderful feeling of confidence that I had never known before. I had always felt since childhood that a relationship could only be complete if it was a learning process, and so it was with Bailey.

We began jokingly to talk about marriage. It represented nothing dramatically new for our relationship, unlike living together, but the commitment did express the certainty of our feelings. A marriage certificate would also be an extraordinary practical blessing because my problems with immigration and visas had developed into a constant nagging worry. On the other hand, I was determined not to change my

Getting married: St Pancras registry office, 3 November 1975. It was a freezing day and I was so unsuitably dressed in my flimsy Hawaiian clothes that Tina Chow, one of the witnesses, had to put her own coat over my shoulders.

name. Bailey found this hard to understand. For me, it was a perfectly straightforward question. Helvin sounded better than Bailey. Besides, I had never liked the idea of compulsorily taking a man's name. I also knew that I would become a prime target for resentment if I began to go around introducing myself to art directors as Mrs Bailey. Even some of the people closest to us managed to give the impression that I should see myself simply as an insignificant attachment to the master. On the morning of the wedding, his secretary expressed surprise that I knew I was getting married, as though I was being done a huge favour.

Both Bailey and I wanted the wedding to be a private occasion without the press. It was a freezing, grey London day in early November 1975. I wore a flimsy silk dress with orchids in my hair and open sandals, which I considered perfectly normal, but caused great mirth among some of the guests. In the evening we had a quiet dinner with friends, given by Michael and Tina Chow, our witnesses.

A few weeks later we stopped by in Honolulu. My mother arranged a party for us, a wonderful Hawaiian occasion peppered with emotion and pride, high farce and one acute social embarrassment. Bailey, as usual, looked as though his clothes were falling apart at the seams. He hated his ceremonial lei of scented maile leaves and kept furtively trying to slip it off whenever he thought he could get away with it, but every time a well-meaning Hawaiian friend would put it back round his neck. Paul and Linda McCartney had also been able to come to the party on their way back from Japan and, since I was very worried that they might be bored, I had told my family to make sure they had fun. Somewhere the wires got crossed. At one ghastly moment I turned round to find one of my mother's friends – male –

Marriage Hawaiian style: Honolulu, November 1975. This time, at least, my clothes were suitable, but Bailey's most certainly weren't.

happily perched on Paul's knee for a celebrity snap. I positively winced, then removed him as fast as possible. We stayed for several weeks and had a marvellous time, my pleasure at taking Bailey home tinged only by my worry that he was bored. I knew he found Hawaii antiseptically American, lacking in the rough magic and intellectual stimulus he found in places with a stronger indigenous culture.

In the early years, I cared so much about pleasing him. He was constantly encouraging me to find more confidence in myself, and I would do anything rather than let him down. Once we were caught in a storm in Tahiti in a small ten-foot whaler. The prow of the boat slapped down between the enormous waves, then lurched sickeningly back until it was swamped by the next curving wall of water. Bailey was sitting up at the front, playing macho adventurer; the fashion editor was crying with fear. I was petrified, but whenever Bailey turned to look at me, I threw back my head and laughed as if I was carried away by the thrill of the moment. Later he said he had known then he would never regret marrying me. Little did he know my real feelings.

My desire to please also led me to behave in ways which now appal and amuse me. For the first year or so, when we had open house and the doorbell rang all day long, I would rush off into the kitchen, at all hours of the day and night, to prepare cocktails, cut up fresh pineapple or make some other little Hawaiian snack, to offer guests. For me this was simply hospitality. However, I was hopeless at cooking, especially meat, since I was pretty much a vegetarian, like Bailey. Fortunately, Cezar loved spontaneity and turned out meals at the drop of a hat. Occasionally, however, I would feel I ought to cook a steak for a friend. I developed a foolproof method: I would shake it from the packet on to a plate and put it into the oven – out of my sight – as fast as possible, until it looked suitably leathery with curly edges. Such specially favoured friends probably prayed Cezar was going to do the cooking.

I was a child bride who grew up within the marriage. My anxieties were largely self-inflicted. I had been so undeveloped with regard to almost every aspect of culture and Bailey made me acutely aware of my lack of an imaginative education. He formed my taste in everything, from music and

The macho adventurer and his reluctant companion.

The top picture was taken in Australia on my first trip abroad for British *Vogue*. I was expecting luxury and first class hotels all the way. When I arrived in Queensland, I discovered that Bailey and I were to be sharing a tiny bedsit with the fashion editor and travel writer. Bailey and I ended up sleeping in the kitchen. The picture below was taken on a trip to Tahiti for Italian *Vogue*. As I posed for Bailey in the grounds of the Club Méditerranée, crowds of holidaymakers gathered around him, all set to get their picture of a lifetime. I found it very difficult to keep my cool.

literature to film and travel and even now I still think he is one of the most literary people and natural thinkers I have ever met. He encouraged me to read from his enormous library: Greene, Marquez and Woolf became firm favourites. For the first time, I felt the pleasure of mentally stretching myself outside my work and questioning my own and others' assumptions. We would sit for hours arguing over a book or a painting and, as I slowly became articulate about my ideas, we began to discuss things on equal terms. Nevertheless, sometimes I felt knocked back by his cynicism at ideas or experiences I found new and exciting. I also remember feeling astounded the first time I knew for sure that Bailey was misinformed, and I think Bailey was equally shocked to hear my voice in disagreement.

Bailey gave me so many cameras over the years, too, thinking I might have a hidden urge to photograph, but I really hate doing things I cannot do well and it felt absurd when I could have much more fun in front of the camera. Nevertheless, we shared so much through work. We were always bouncing around ideas and our complementary bond with the camera gave us a mutual understanding of the quirks produced by the peculiarities attached to our trade. Jerry Hall once told me how lucky it was that Mick Jagger, as a performer, instinctively understood why she needed the reassurance of his compliments when she was away from the catwalk. In the same way, I never had to explain to Bailey why I glanced into mirrors and he did not have to explain to me why he took his camera with him when he went down to the corner shop or slept with it beside the bed.

We were so content that we began to withdraw from the world. At first we kept virtually open house and evenings alone were a rare luxury. Then, after a couple of years, we began to leave the door unanswered in the evenings and to guard the weekends more jealously. We added another floor at the top of the house where Bailey would paint and I would read. Bailey built a darkroom and would print all day Saturday; I simply enjoyed my own company. It was wonderful to be on our own. Both Bailey and I loathed the clubbing life – although I like to go out on the town with friends once in a blue moon – but many were the evenings we spent entertaining more lively friends sitting mutely in the corner of a seedy disco or dingy nightclub trying not to look too bored.

Our own trips abroad were very different. For Bailey, travel meant exploring a country to capture it in his camera, and roughing it in the process. Every summer we would take off for a couple of months with our passports, money and two small bags of clothes: Bailey had his cameras, and I had one drip-dry dress for emergencies. We journeyed like snails, very slowly, halting all the time, which gave me a wonderfully close, detailed view of the landscapes and cultures through which we passed: India and North Africa, Tahiti and Haiti, Australia and America . . . The list is endless. Bailey's continual curiosity, determination and sense of discovery gave every trip memorable moments.

In the end, though, I tired of the travelling. It was exciting the first time and fun the second time, but third time around it was plain hard work. Living out of a shopping bag of clothes, remaining constantly on the move for two months and thinking always in terms of the camera is not my idea of a holiday. I am the kind of person who likes clean hotel rooms, lavatories that work and water you can drink. Bailey found it hard to do nothing. He does not like the sun or the sea. His idea of sport is playing chess next to an open window and his version of swimming was floating on his back or, if he wanted to do something really strenuous, treading water. I, by contrast, longed to lie in the sun and flop around in a swimming pool or on a beach for a few weeks with my family.

And so we began to take our summer trips separately. I had several marvellous summers in Hawaii. Suzon, Naomi and I would spend a few blissful months rediscovering shared childhood pleasures and irritating Steve by recalling embarrassing baby tales. Suzon and I had remained especially close. My parents had by now gone separate ways, but they were still the closest of friends. There was never a question of our having to take sides or of losing contact with either of them and their marriage was simply replaced by a teasing affection. For a long time I was the only one who had cut loose while Suzon hung out in Honolulu, experimenting with alternative life styles. Then we became scattered far and wide. Suzon divided her time between Bali and Jamaica, where she and her boyfriend, Jesse, ran a café in Negril. Naomi was living in Morocco married to a French diplomat – although stubbornly resisting the role of the diplomat's wife – and Steve still lived with my mother. He had grown up into a beguilingly generous but lazy beachbum. One sibling or another was always visiting. Occasionally there were incidents which still produced in me the full blast of elder sisterly fury, as when Steve blew the allowance he had been earning by helping Bailey's assistant on a ridiculous pair of leather trousers.

In those good years, Bailey and I were both mature enough to enjoy what we had and not look into the future. No matter how strong love is, there has to be a rational recognition that you cannot count on anything lasting forever. Nevertheless, our marriage was founded on certain fundamental points of sanity: although we sometimes argued, we never fought, and neither of us nurtured jealousies. Bailey's friends seemed to find this difficult to believe, perhaps because he had such a reputation for being a temperamental dictator at work. I remember several times having to persuade friends it was true, once after I had accused him of being tone-deaf and they had automatically assumed this would turn into an almighty marital flare-up. In our terms it was not even grounds for a discussion. Bailey is tone-deaf.

My girlfriends, on the other hand, found it difficult to understand my lack of resentment of Bailey's former women. He had remained in contact with all his ex-girlfriends and ex-wives – except for his first wife Rosemary – and they have always been the only women he considered his good friends. At first I did find it hard to live up to my image of their beauty and intelligence, but I enjoy the friendship and company of women so much that I would have felt that I had missed out if I had not known them.

What we all have in common, I think, is the love of laughter. Jean has the most peaceful temperament. She had always hated the bright lights according to Bailey, and by the time I came along had retreated to the rural life in Cornwall where she runs a hotel with her husband. Catherine, on the other hand, has the most natural cool. Most of all, though, I wanted to meet Penelope. Cezar had adored her and had a fund of hilarious stories about the way she would come home with anything from a Tibetan holy man to the entire Black Panther Group. Bailey became so accustomed to finding strangers in the house while they lived together that a homeless party guest once managed to move into the spare bedroom for two weeks before anyone noticed. Penelope stayed out of contact for a year after she and Bailey broke up, but when we got married she sent a telegram, and when we finally met after another year, we got on like a house on fire, although intellectually she is light years ahead of me.

Role reversal: Bailey with his favourite cockatoo, photographed by Mrs Bailey. The commission came from the *Sunday Times* on the memorable occasion of Bailey being voted the worst-dressed man in England.

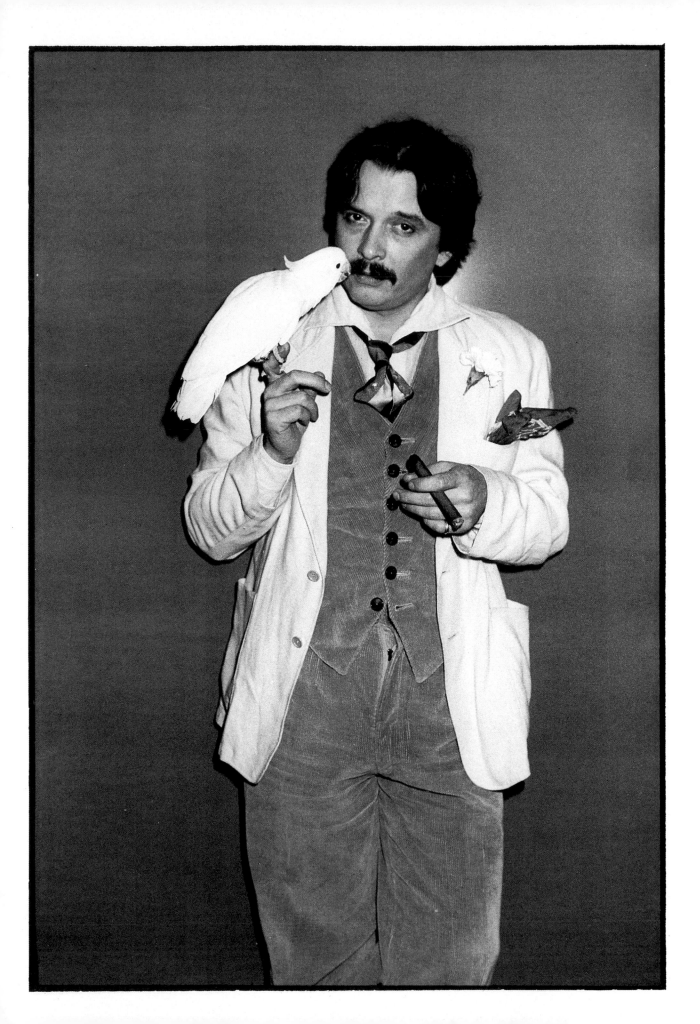

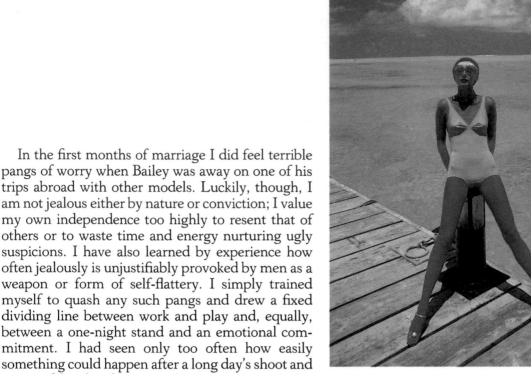

The finished shots were fantastic because of the colours, but I felt a fool at the time, wearing a blonde wig and coloured tights in a completely natural Tahitian setting.

In the first months of marriage I did feel terrible pangs of worry when Bailey was away on one of his trips abroad with other models. Luckily, though, I am not jealous either by nature or conviction; I value my own independence too highly to resent that of others or to waste time and energy nurturing ugly suspicions. I have also learned by experience how often jealously is unjustifiably provoked by men as a weapon or form of self-flattery. I simply trained myself to quash any such pangs and drew a fixed dividing line between work and play and, equally, between a one-night stand and an emotional commitment. I had seen only too often how easily something could happen after a long day's shoot and a second bottle of wine in the evening, but I also knew how little it meant. Eventually, I refused to go on working trips with Bailey unless I was in the shot because I felt that my presence set up a triangle of tension which created difficulties and unnecessary strain.

Nevertheless, we worked together a lot of the time. Living and working with Bailey considerably honed my sensibilities as a model and gave me an enviable power to be choosy about my work. After a year or so, I stopped doing shots with other models. It was not a question of acting the star, simply that it had always been difficult to balance my looks, which produced disappointing results for everyone. The constant changes in Bailey's work – he began to do far more continuity sequences for example – added a lot to my own. Sometimes I wonder what Bailey would do if he could not take photographs. He never stops experimenting and never will, not because he is a workaholic, but because the camera is like an extension of his senses. Later he began to give more and more of his time to painting, but in those days he was nearly always printing or taking photographs on Saturdays. That was how the nudes in *Trouble and Strife* began. Bailey was interested by the book I had done with Shinoyama, but the shots we began to do soon after we were married were far more random, only a part of his continual experimenting and certainly never planned as a sequence for publication. They built up over the course of seven years: some were taken on our trips abroad, others in the house on Saturdays.

They were highly personal photographs, but not in the sexual sense. In fact all the calculated erotic shots, with lacy lingerie, silk stockings and unzipped leather, were fashion commissions taken in quite a different spirit. For the more private photographs, I was often asleep or sunbathing, and for many of the poses I was still bleary-eyed from a lazy Saturday

Portrait Left: by Helmut Newton.

morning or fresh from the washing up. Bailey would often have an idea, set up the shot and then grab me for only a few minutes. For me, the personal element came in the settings, the props and the jokes. They appear in many of the photographs I like best: the very first one, in which I am blowing bubble gum, or those with old friends like my cats and the exercise bike. For Bailey, I suppose, the personal side came through the photography itself, the imagery and symbolism with which he portrayed my character or depicted me as everywoman. The problem was that he never explained that to me: he did not tell me, for example, why he wanted me to walk into our bedroom naked with a breakfast tray and a towel around my head, or to lie on the studio floor wrapped like a mummy in newspaper with only my pubic hair showing. I hated that photograph.

Although I was happy to strip like that for him, privately, I was upset by the idea of the photographs being published. When Bailey initially told me about the book, I made no attempt to stop him because I really did not

Portrait Right: by Patrick Lichfield for his book *The Most Beautiful Women*. Bailey was the only man in the book.

Although I dislike the paparazzi converging on their victims at moments of privacy, I have learned that there is never any point in getting angry with the press — they are too powerful and you need them on your side. Most of the time, anyway, the crime is no worse than silliness — once I made a passing joke about sex being good for you and I was not allowed to forget it for months. While Bailey and I were separating I found it less easy to be philosophical about them. However, on the whole, my strategy is simply to laugh, say as little as possible and tape record all interviews.

believe he could have found a publisher, especially since narrative nudes were not at that time being done in England. Suddenly, it was too late and the pictures had all been sent to the publisher. That was my fault. On the other hand, I was angry that I had not been allowed to decide how, and for whom, I stripped. We argued. Bailey maintained that I would inevitably have chosen the flattering portraits and that there was no justification for publishing such a book. I nevertheless felt I should have been allowed to choose.

Bailey had removed from me the crucial element of control; for commissioned shots I always knew the terms of publication at the time the photograph was taken and could refuse anything I felt debased my image or that of women generally. I have always felt very strongly that a woman does not debase herself simply by removing her clothes for the camera, but the issues are subtler and I always considered them carefully. Firstly, I find images which fail to acknowledge the sexuality of women and depict them as romantic weaklings far more offensive than, for example, the strong, overtly sexual women in Helmut Newton's pictures. His women are aware that they are being surveyed and openly express their response, whether it is one of pleasure or aggression. Secondly, the role of the woman always depends on the specific photograph. Bailey has always maintained that all good fashion photographers have a homosexual streak which takes the depiction of a woman beyond sexual attraction to affection and understanding. He includes himself in that description: he has always said he wants the women in his photographs to be in control of their own destinies and bodies – beyond the reach of man's wallet and sexual desire.

Finally, interpretation must rest with the eye of the beholder. My greatest worry at the time about *Trouble and Strife* was that women would feel I had allowed myself to be portrayed as a sexual object and identify me with the kind of girlie photograph or advertising shot that I most dislike. Now, in fact, I no longer feel that and the book has become something of which I feel proud although the newspaper and pubic hair photograph still gives me the shivers. In retrospect, I should have guessed that the only unpleasant reaction would be masculine – from a male journalist who asked me how I felt when I thought of the way men would be using the photographs. The idea appalled me at the time. Now I would reply that men have always disregarded the images women want to offer of themselves – even the way they dress or walk down the street – and used them for their own purposes, and that it is better to try and teach them new ways of seeing than to deny that our bodies and sexuality exist.

Looking back on our relationship, it was a mistake for Bailey and I to spend so much time apart – sometimes as much as five to six months of the year. At the time that was hard to see because I was so idealistic about wanting a modern marriage. But it definitely gave me a curious sense of emotional detachment: I began, for the first time, to look at Bailey with a critical eye and to acknowledge that sometimes I had good reasons to think differently from him. But if I stopped hero-worshipping him and felt in a sense that perfection had slipped away, I still loved him very deeply and remained very contented with what we shared.

Then, like a stone shattering glassy water, the death of Suzon broke the smooth surface of my spoilt existence. Bailey broke the news to me. We had just returned from a working trip to Paris. Shortly after we arrived in the house the power went dead. Then the telephone rang. Bailey talked for some time. He hung up and told me it had been Suzon's boyfriend. She had

The perfect shot for the paparazzi, at the opening of the exhibition for *Trouble and Strife*. And one of my favourite shots (right) from that book, taken in a hotel room in southern India. I had barely woken up and Bailey just rearranged me slightly in my sleep.

been cycling along the coastal road above Negril when her bicycle had slipped, and she had fallen over the cliff. She had fallen badly and suffered fatal head injuries. She was dead.

For a few seconds, I remained suspended in a limbo of disbelief. Then, desperately hoping that I had heard the wrong name, the meaning of the words began to seep through and I became hysterical. When I was too drained to cry any more, I sat simply stunned and confused. My brain had recorded the statement of the facts, but could not think through the reality: I would never see Suzon again, one of the people I most cared for in the world had died. As the periods of hysteria became shorter, the spaces of blank confusion grew longer.

I flew to Honolulu. Suzon had to be cremated in Jamaica, but her ashes were sent home and we took them out to sea for a very simple service. The administration and processing of the body jarred horribly on my spirit: I felt sick when the box containing Suzon's ashes was banged clumsily down in front of us at the airport. We took it home and I removed the jar from the box. Wherever I put it was wrong: the kitchen table unclean, the living room grotesque, the bedroom insulting. Death did not fit in the house.

The exhausting tension of grief was punctuated by an occasional sense of the ridiculous which broke through the suspended animation of everyday life. Steve refused to wear a clean aloha shirt or the ginger lei I had arranged for the service and we had a terrible fight; at the crucial moment of the service my mother was unable to get the top off the urn to scatter the ashes. The minister looked pained, and started banging the urn against the side of the boat. We laughed, slightly hysterically, as the bleakness was momentarily ousted, then veered wildly back to tears. The giddy elation of momentary release from grief made the turn to the pain even sharper. That was the first time I ever saw my father cry.

The longest plunge was my return to England. I could no longer contain or isolate the pain on the other side of the world. It became less sharp, but more difficult to bear as the confusion dropped away and I began to distinguish clear troughs of sadness which lengthened and spread outwards to engulf every part of my daily existence. I went into a deep depression for two years. I saw friends and I continued with my work, but I had nothing to give to either. The pain was too strong. Bailey was my closest, most caring friend during this time: he had broken the news to my family, and had taken me away to the Yucatan on my way back from Hawaii for the worst wounds to heal. Yet by nature he shied away from death and instinctively he wanted to protect me from it rather than help me explore it. We never talked of Suzon. I could not bear to go to the guest room where she had stayed. I could not even find her in my dreams. I felt, completely unfairly, resentful that Bailey had not come to Hawaii for the service. It must have been hard to live with me then.

I bottled up the horror and began to feel obsessed by death. My mind ran on two separate tracks, the trivia of everyday life that ticked on around me and the questions raised by Suzon's death. It challenged everything in which I had trusted. The strange events of the day of Suzon's death re-ran themselves in my memory a thousand times. I had been quarrelsome and Bailey had been mysteriously overcome by physical nausea; in the car from the airport a curious image of my family gathered together without Bailey and Suzon had suddenly flashed through my mind, like a film still. I became convinced that I, not Suzon, had been meant to die, and that she had taken my place.

Suzon Lee Helvin.

I felt, not as the result of any conscious decision, but from a sense of indisputable knowledge, that the sole guideline in which I could trust was to behave in all things, even the smallest details of life, in a way that would make Suzon happy – that I had been living on false premises and that I must learn new ones which distinguished the essential from the trivial. As the suffering dug deeper in my heart, so I wanted to rise higher in my life. Anything which distracted from that I cast aside with an almost dispassionate clarity.

Then, after more than two years, I finally felt a sense of catharsis, a conviction that I could draw something positive from the horror and that I had the strength to do so. I began to look very harshly at my own life and tried to be brutally honest with myself. I had become a robot within my work and I decided to move out of mainstream modelling. I knew also that before Suzon's death I had been a spoilt brat; now I might still be spoilt, but I could no longer be a brat.

One day Bailey told me I had changed. He was right: I had always had a mind of my own, but it was only at the age of twenty-seven that I finally began to use it. I had finally grown up. The reflection of myself I saw in his eyes, however, was still that of a child. He did not want to know the woman who perceived him in quite a different way. For all those years I had admired him so much that it was difficult to think of him as a man with emotions and frailties. Now, I began to see the immaturities and selfishness that are in us all.

Our separation was years coming, but we had parted emotionally long before I left the bedroom. The love remained, but the element of physical passion died. I had one brief affair, an expression of my unhappiness, which

I chose to end for my love for Bailey; he had many meaningless flings. Two people leave each other. Yet the breakdown had nothing to do with fidelity. Now, when I was both more vulnerable and more honest, I found his strength of personality – something I had once needed – domineering. I was no longer prepared to put energy into his need for reassurance.

The parting became inevitable, but I found it difficult to face the fact that we could not make the marriage work again if we tried. My thoughts crystallized during a visit to Hawaii, and on my return I discussed my feelings with Bailey. I still wanted our relationship as man and wife, but I needed him to help me make it work. But he simply did not want to know: he would not admit that there was any wrong on his side and blamed everything on the way I had changed. I knew that was a reflection of his own difficulties and self-deception. But nevertheless it was up to me to find the solution alone. At that point I gave up. It was difficult for us both, but it was all very controlled. There were tears, but there was no screaming. I caused the break-up, but we both took the final decision. I simply moved upstairs. Late in the autumn of 1983, I started sleeping in the guest room. I never went back. It was a relief, but it was also devastating to realize there was nothing I could do. I hated the way things seemed to be ending; I worried for the future and I became physically ill.

For a long time – over six months – the press discovered nothing. There was little evidence. I stayed in the house. On the surface little had changed: we still often went out together to the cinema or a restaurant. Some people, especially male friends, found our *ménage* hard to understand, but there was no reason to move out, Bailey was away so much that the house felt almost more my home than his, and I had known, through the continuing warmth of my parents' friendship and Bailey's affection for his ex-wives, that it was possible for us to live together happily as friends. The laughter remained. He would still wake me in the morning by calling me a rude name, and I would still tell him he was the scruffiest man in Primrose Hill. He still gave me his 'invaluable' advice. When I was trying to learn a few phrases of Indonesian before I went to visit my foster child there, he told me I was wasting my time. The only phrase I needed to know for my encounters with slave-traders was 'My husband will not pay'.

When the press finally discovered that the marriage was over they completely misunderstood. I publicly surfaced with another man, who I had started seeing more than six months after I had left Bailey's bed. They assumed that was the cause of the problems and possibly even news to Bailey. Once we escaped from a restaurant by climbing over a wall at the back and sneaking out through the shop next door. After we allowed ourselves to be photographed, but refused to pay the press any attention, they soon lost interest.

I think that for a long time Bailey hoped I would move back to his side; he had once joked in the early days that we should divorce and remarry. I knew, however, that would never be so, and I began to sense that the longer I stayed in the house the more difficult the final parting would be. I felt that I should move out in order to make a clean break. For Bailey, that was the real divorce, and very hard to accept. Almost despite himself he wanted to control the terms of my departure and, since I needed his financial help to buy my own home, he had the means to do so. It was a very difficult time, which dragged on for months, and I hated the moments of friction. Once we flew at each other. I was wound up like a spring with tension at the time and I said things I bitterly regret. But it did clear the air.

The laughter has always remained – captured here by Jacques Henri Lartigue.

Our relaxed attitudes contradicted the ground rules of suspicion on which legal separation and divorce are based, and our relationship followed two quite separate strands: we always discussed problems in a very relaxed, friendly way at home, yet things immediately became acrimonious whenever the lawyers were involved. At one point Bailey instructed his lawyer to have no contact with mine, at another the flat was going to be in his name and finally it was going to be contingent on my remaining single. Putting affairs of the heart on paper seemed to distort them out of all recognition. It was hard to be sure which level represented the truth.

Now that everything has been resolved I know in my heart that only good will come out of divorce for both of us. We remain inextricably linked by a strange bond of the spirit, as strong and rare as that between a blood brother and sister. The passion will always remain: I would still do anything for Bailey and I know he would for me. We believe in each other. Sometimes I have a strange, occasionally frightening, feeling that I will be seeing or hearing from him every day of my life.

C A T W A L K

I am not a showgirl at heart, but the catwalk fascinates me. It is not the thrill of an ecstatic audience, although I have felt the exhilaration of those moments: the passion and elation, the blaze of the lights and the challenge of stepping out alone before a crowd of thousands. Nor is it the lure of the money: at times I have valued it and at others I have turned down thousands of dollars. In the end it is the excitement of being at the pivot of the business I know and love. It is on the catwalk that money and art meet. When I step out before an audience, I am not parading myself, nor displaying beautiful clothes. I am selling them.

It is that chemistry between art and business which still makes Paris the capital of the fashion industry. *Haute couture*, that indefinably French concept, could have been born nowhere else. Where, outside France, has fashion always commanded the social respect and government support essential for it to thrive? Where else have designers always been able to live as part of a cosmopolitan community bringing together the worlds of art and commerce, literature and politics? Today, of course, the money lies in ready-to-wear – fashion fitting the international culture of time, money and mass communications – but the institutions and sense of honour attached to *haute couture* survive. The Chambre Syndicale de la Haute Couture, founded in the thirties, still watches over the designers, bestowing upon the few who can meet its strict standards the coveted title of Grand Couturier. It is their code, drawn up over fifty years ago, which laid down the ground rules that have now acquired the mystique of time-honoured tradition: twice a year, in January and July, every couturier should display to his customers a limited number of designs for the coming season. Attendance at the shows was to be by invitation only to prevent access by copyists.

Twenty years later, in the fifties, the first licensing agreements were drawn up around Paris *haute couture*, allowing companies to manufacture and sell articles under a designer's name. Since then the industry has changed beyond all recognition. In America, a designer label now sells anything from blue jeans to wine and chocolates, and 'Fashion Ave.' grosses $900 billion a year. Fashion has also become Italy's major industry. In Japan, where the boundaries with art have always been less rigid, Issey Miyake has been a national hero for years and Kenzo Takada of Jap is said to be worth over $20,000,000. Meanwhile, back in France, where it all started, the cultural cachet has survived the transition to mass marketing. Through Pierre Cardin, the king of licensing, *haute couture* has finally met *haute cuisine*: he now owns Maxim's. Yves St Laurent may start to license cigarettes, and André Courrèges has designed car hubcaps which won him a Japanese industrial award. French overseas sales are worth 12 billion

On the catwalk all appears to be serene composure, but backstage there is often a chaotic madhouse, with dressers and design assistants pushing the models to get them back on the catwalk within thirty seconds.

francs and the net continues to widen. As the financial stakes get higher, attendant problems creep in; for every Calvin Klein, Kenzo or Yves St Laurent original, hundreds of copies will appear around the world. Bootlegging is growing at a fantastic pace and designers are beginning to sew on their labels statements of copyright. Litigation is multiplying every year and the designers make sure they will win.

As a result, the individually fitted and painstakingly made gowns of *haute couture*, once seen at every salon and soirée, have been ousted by clothes made quickly on the cutting table, not on the body, to a pattern of standard size. But these are sold in the same way, two months after the *haute couture* weeks, in March and October, to enormous audiences of fashion buyers from all over the world. They set the trends for the coming year and determine what the customer will be offered. *Haute couture*, by comparison, has to be heavily sponsored and always runs at a deficit. But it remains as essential as ever to the fashion industry: the clothes are not simply outrageously expensive garments for a small elite, but prestige and glamour for the whole industry.

To my mind the pleasure of show-modelling *haute couture* lies not so much in the show as the chance to observe the practice of the skills which make fashion. The model provides the body around which a handmade dress is constructed and watches it grow from the original inspiration and raw materials to the finished article as each part is meticulously fitted, and

then sewn into shape by the seamstress before finally being checked and finished with immaculate detail. I always felt a sense of privilege to be involved in the production processes of the applied art from which the business has grown.

I felt a similar sense of honour to be on the catwalk. Showing *haute couture* needs quite distinct skills from those of the camera model and the ready-to-wear catwalker: photogenic beauty and the showgirl instinct count for little compared to the knack of wearing clothes. It may sound ridiculously easy, but it is in reality extraordinarily difficult to capture the grace and movement to match the aesthetics of the clothes and to display every detail to the prospective customer. For this reason, it is a world apart. Every couturier has his own *cabine* girls, who know perfectly how to show his clothes, and who continue to show them at his salon after collections week is over. But for the week when buyers and the press flood in from all over the world, the designer will hire perhaps half a dozen other top show models or, very occasionally, a personality or photographic model who knows how to move and suits his image. She becomes very much identified with his look.

For five years I was lucky enough to model *haute couture* for Yves St Laurent. He is, for me, quite simply the best. His construction is perfect, his eye for colour marvellous and his control and authority evident in the confidence with which he combines ideas yet always turns out a completely balanced total look. The originality and wit behind each of the collections I modelled never ceased to amaze me: for each he would draw on cultural sources and play with the styles of the great designers of the past with astonishing verve. One year it was an *homage* to Picasso and another year the inspiration came from the Ballet Russe: one year the ethnic influence was North African, another Mandarin Chinese. In the year the Mittérand government came to power and the Minister of Culture, Jack Lang, allowed the collections to take place in the Musée du Louvre, the bridal dress, the traditional climax of the show, was studded with a single red socialist rose. It was a classic St Laurent touch.

Yves learned his skills at Dior where he was forced into the limelight by Dior's sudden death in 1957, redesigning the spring collection with spectacular success. After disappearing to do national military service, he reappeared on his own as the first Paris designer to take ready-to-wear seriously, but still produce immaculate *haute couture*. His perfectionism is perfectly measured by the week of fittings running up to the shows. Initial fittings are always done by seamstresses, who are junior designers specializing in evening dresses or daywear, skirts, trousers or suits, but everything has to be correct at each fitting, including hair and make-up, so that the design works towards a finished look. Each year I was surprised again by how much there was to consider: the nature of the fabric and the way it falls, the cut and length of each garment, the neckline and sleeves, the zippers and stitching.

Then would come the penultimate fitting, a dispassionate and relentless grilling, the fashion equivalent of an MI5 vetting. We would enter the plush red show room in the St Laurent salon in strict order of turn: in the centre would be Yves, flanked on either side by his senior assistants, Loulou de la Falaise and Madame Munoz, with Pierre Bergé sitting behind them. Berge, who met Yves at Dior, has become the *éminence grise* behind the marketing operation, a newspaper magnate and millionaire who is a name to conjure with in fashion circles. At the back would be a small army of assistants scribbling down notes of all the necessary alterations and, unfortunately, Yves's chihuahua. He hated the models and always saved an embarrassingly loud growl for me. The feeling was mutual. Perhaps he saw himself as a watchdog over the secrets of the collection.

The final fitting was far more enjoyable. Yves would first minutely examine every fold, zip and seam, then effect extraordinary transformations by accessorizing the outfits in different ways, with flowers and feathers, gloves, jewellery and hair ornaments. It was a lesson in the aesthetics of fashion. Finally, a Polaroid snap would be taken as a guide for the show, the chosen accessories would be neatly tied in a plastic bag and everything attached to the dress.

The show itself was always feverishly exciting, yet still leisurely and closely watched, an extension of the designer's precise and exact craft. The essence of *haute couture* catwalk is simplicity, to allow the clothes to speak for themselves. The models always use the classic Dior walk, with slightly slanted back and hunched shoulders, to allow the perfection of detail and execution to be closely studied. Closest to the catwalk, only a few feet away, are the front row group of *femmes du monde* and *femmes à la mode* – in Yves's case, Catherine Deneuve, Paloma Picasso, the Rothschilds and Hélène Rochas – who can afford a dress costing upwards of $5,000 and provide a walking showcase for the designer. Gathered around the end of the catwalk, elbowing each other out of the way, are the representatives of the other world: the film crews and press who photograph and write fashion news. For that publicity alone, the industry is indebted to *haute couture*: as the dependent child of mass marketing, ready-to-wear thrives on reflected prestige and high-profile news coverage.

That mass marketing of fashion has redrawn the fashion map. America and Italy have grown enormously through the ready-to-wear stars who emerged in the seventies – on the one hand, Perry Ellis, Ralph Lauren and Calvin Klein, who did so much with clothes suited to the life style of American women, and on the other Armani, Versace, Ferré and the Italian knitwear designers based around Milan, who have founded empires through superb marketing as well as sleek design.

Tokyo fashion has already boomed, but it visibly lacks the co-ordination provided by a professional body; at one time, the collections in Japan drifted on over the space of ten weeks.

London has not benefited in the same way, despite the endlessly original ideas bubbling up from their designers all the time, and in the seventies it hardly figured on the buyers' map or calendar. Bailey always says the British invent fashion, the French copy it and the Italians market it. Certainly, the British fail to capitalize on the talent coming through the art schools. What makes the situation even more ridiculous is that the area of the market in which they are so strong – young street-fashion – is also one in which they have no competition. The disparity between talent and money is the result of the long-standing lack of government encouragement or subsidy and, perhaps, too, that deep-rooted English *malaise* and social stigma attached to selling your work. But it became far worse when the bucks began to get so much bigger because fashion collections became an enterprise requiring enormous amounts of capital impossible for small unsubsidised designers to raise. The recent resurgence of London through Katherine Hammet, Betty Jackson and Body Map has opened up another chance for London to get the position it deserves. The buyers are beginning to return, but there is still a long way to go.

Paris, however, remains prestige city: It is always *en avant* as they say. Everybody shows and everybody comes. In the audience will be fashion editors from every city and buyers from every store – the boys from Bloomingdales in New York, Seibu in Tokyo, Harrods in London and dear old Liberty House in Honolulu. Paris is also the mecca of the catwalk world: it draws the top hairdressers and the best make-up people. When I began, a trip across the Atlantic was an event and the catwalk was a parochial world. But now a hairdresser flies in from New York and a make-up artist from Tokyo, and the dedicated show model commutes around the world, twice a year, starting in Milan and moving on to Paris, London, New York and Tokyo. The pace is faster and the pressures much greater: to succeed, a model must excel everywhere.

The social geography of the catwalk has also changed out of all recognition since I first tripped on to the catwalk in the early seventies. Where ready-to-wear show work was distinctly down-market in the sixties, particularly in England, the problem now is not to find the girls, but to winnow out those who know how to move from the stick insects and to pay the personality models who bring the press flocking in and sell the clothes. The showgirl has always been socially acceptable in France and America, since Patou shipped American society beauties to Paris in the twenties, but in England she went through a bad slump in the fifties, ousted by John French's photographic stars who emerged through high fashion filtering into mass circulation papers, and that continued through the sixties.

It was only in the mid-seventies that live fashion turned into show biz and the showgirl became a star again. Valentino flew in Brooke Shields to model his collection. Iman, the wonderful Somalian model, was paid $7,000 for half an hour on the catwalk in Munich and was taken to and from the show in a police-escorted limousine. And the general rates of pay went spiralling upwards. Everything is counted in dollars, now, of course. A top girl can pretty much name her fee, but will expect around $1,000 for an hour show in Milan and perhaps a little more in Paris. In New York, where things are still done by the clock, it is $400 an hour. After commission and taxes you end up with less than two-thirds of that, but it is still good money – and you can always do straight cash deals. London pays very badly, probably about ten years behind New York, so it hardly sees top showgirls; Tokyo is good money and there is an endless market for the European look, but it has a very high cost of living.

The show biz arrived when the French designers discovered fashion as theatre. They discovered it through Kenzo, who brought it to Paris first as a fringe cultural event and then in a mainstream spring show entitled 'Cover Girls'. That show changed the entire concept of the way clothes could be shown. Kenzo substituted a round stage for a runway, a light show for white film lights, photographic models for showgirls and, most important of all, complete spontaneity for the static mannequin parade which was *de rigueur* at the time. I was lucky enough to be in that show and it was a fantastic experience. Kenzo has always loved exuberance and he stipulated only that we should enjoy ourselves and look happy. The girls went wild, clowning and somersaulting, doing the rhumba and dancing the can-can, showering each other with feather-like confetti, waving sparklers and baring their breasts like the girls on Rue St Denis.

In some ways, Kenzo was drawing on spectacle as it had been used in Japanese fashion for many years. But there were several crucial differences. One was the switch from strictly choreographed movement to improvis-

Four different outfits from the ready-to-wear collections in one Paris season: they show the importance of the Total Look and meticulous attention to detail. The top two outfits were designed by Yves St Laurent, the bottom left by Claude Montana and the bottom right by Karl Lagerfeld.

ation; the other was the audience. Kenzo had the nerve to put on the show, not in Tokyo, not even as Yamamoto had done in London, but in the most hallowed enclave of them all. The sophisticated Paris audience had never seen anything like it before, and they stood and roared. What Kenzo had grasped was that ready-to-wear needed to be shown as a popular fashion statement, not simply as a down-market imitation of *haute couture*. The volatile elation of an audience of three thousand packed into a huge tent needed the sense of an event. Since the shows had become theatre on a huge scale, they needed to be extravaganzas which stirred every sense, with the most beautiful girls and clothes, and the very best in sound and lighting.

After 'Cover Girls' there were no hard and fast rules for catwalking. There were a few rather faddish phases: first came the wild look, next a dancey style, then a patch with vampy solos half way down the runway. Every designer had his preferences, but all models needed energy and verve, and the ability to act the part. The *enfants terribles* of the design scene were the most outrageous: Thierry Mugler liked punkish models with a very sexy walk and lots of improvised craziness and Claude Montana wanted deadpan eeriness, which always gave me terrible giggles. I could not help seeing myself as a fifties B-movie body-snatcher. Yves still wanted absolute control and a more classic line, but he used the element of spectacle in a very inspirational way. Once, he saw me as Carmen and that became the theme for half of an enormous two-hour show. Towards the end of the seventies, catwalking found its most aggressive and distinctly unglamorous style at the World's End in London, where the designers were trying to provoke the new approach needed by their designs.

The use of fashion theatre to disrupt expectation is a well-founded tradition: Dior used it in the late fifties, Quant in the early sixties and Issey Miyake, in the seventies, organized a show in Tokyo for an audience of 12,000 to try and create a new understanding of clothes among the buying public. Over ten years later, theatre on the same scale reached Paris, through Thierry Mugler who turned his 1984 ready-to-wear show into an enormous spectacle produced by a rock impresario, with a cast of fifty and an audience of 6,000. Most significant of all, half the audience were paying ticket-holders. It was the first time that the general public had ever been invited to a live Paris show. That democratization will undoubtedly go further. It is only a small step from the in-house videos of *haute couture* and ready-to-wear shows being mailed to buyers around the world to the fashion show becoming mass entertainment.

The arrival of show biz has done nothing but good for the industry. Yet there is a part of me which regrets the craving for spectacle. Perhaps I am too much of a purist, but sometimes I wish they would stop all the razzmatazz and get on with showing the clothes. After all, that is what everyone is meant to be looking at. As a model, too, I like to concentrate on displaying the clothes rather than performing. Everyday movements are more difficult, if less stressful, than strict choreography, yet I cannot help but feel they are the most honest way of showing. It seems to me to reflect the right philosophy of fashion design – that clothes should be seen in relation to body shape and life style more than to the look for that season.

The Americans have always had a more straighforward approach: there are no spotlights, no drama and the audience sits just a few feet away from the catwalk, sipping coffee and occasionally passing comment to the models. Sometimes I used to feel like an up-market door-to-door saleswoman. The aim never seemed to be to dazzle the audience or captivate their imagination, but to convince the customers they could look as good and feel as comfortable in the clothes as the models. One of the best shows I ever saw was by Calvin Klein, which achieved the same effect for a much larger audience by using thirty stunning photographic girls with very low-key presentation and simple, everyday clothes in different combinations. It made fashion seem so accessible.

That same relaxed feeling always pervaded the calm backstage organization and cossetting sense of comfort of the American shows. Where New York efficiency had seemed so stifling in the studio, it felt gloriously civilized after the pandemonium of French and Italian show timetables. Instead of nervous panic unleashing every swear word under the sun, the designer simply coaxed us on to the stage like a high school sports team. The fearlessness of luxury, too, felt like a breath of fresh air after all that European understatement. Bill Blass, for instance, always showed in the classy elegance of the Pierre Hotel, where we could eat lunch and have a glass of champagne instead of rushing out to grab a croissant and coffee. In Japan, where *obentos*, or lunch-boxes, would be laid on, there were always problems with the raw fish and pickles. Sometimes there were frayed tempers, too, due to language problems. But the show itself was always very rehearsed and organized.

European shows look superb from front-of-house, but backstage they are a madhouse of naked women, dressers and make-up artists, with the designer on the point of collapse from nerves. Sometimes we would be lined up, like battery chickens, on a row of plastic chairs, with the hairdressers on one side and the make-up artist on the other. The atmosphere is always one of expectation but also nerve-racking sponta-

neity. Milan was the worst. Eight or ten shows, each with a different mood, make-up and hair, were packed into a day, and in my day the models were ferried from one auditorium to the next like schoolgirls on an outing, with delays ricochetting through the day once the shows got behind schedule. At least in Paris the shows are mainly in one place – one year in the Tuileries, another year the Louvre, another the Forum des Halles – so that you do not waste half your energy dashing around between shows in a taxi.

Nevertheless, collections week in Paris is pretty wearing. The hotels need a well-planned, strategical approach. Many models' priority is room service to avoid the standard evening ritual of grabbing a cheese baguette – or starving. My priority was always sleep. Bailey and I always insisted on a quiet room because we had often found noise a problem. One year we got our strategy wrong: there was a heat wave and since our room was on the lower floor of a tall building and there was no air, it was like being in a sauna. I woke up in the middle of the night gasping for oxygen and felt around for Bailey. He was not there. When I turned on the light I found him lying on the floor, jammed up against the crack of the door, breathing in the draught from the corridor.

Paris is also, of course, the hub of fashion socializing, unbeatable for cool and razzle. Occasionally it is fun. More often it is just good observation value as a comedy of manners since the designers have social entrées wherever they have clients – from the White House to the oil sheik's palace. An extraordinary selection of artists and bankers, enterpreneurs and journalists, society women and buyers of every currency and nationality always crawl out of the woodwork for collections week. There is also every type of fashion caricature on display, from style elitists to fashion victims

Above: A fashion shot of a Valentino evening suit by Francois Lamy for Italian *Vogue*; the blonde hairpiece sprouting red and purple tufts was designed by Jean Louis David. Photographers working for Italian *Vogue* have always been allowed the creative freedom to shoot the clothes against theatrical backdrops and dramatic special effects.

Right: On location in Bombay, playing the *maharani*.

tricked out in slavish accordance with headquarters' instructions for the season. There is only one topic of conversation – fashion – and the *lingua franca* is French. The socialites score points and stroke each others' egos, while the harried workers – the buyers and journalists who go to literally hundreds of shows a year – exchange information. The gossip-column fodder is pretty indigestible and usually goes with a lot of gasping, fanning and flash-bulbs popping.

The ranking can be gauged quite easily from the audience. Every designer has a big, often aristocratic, name on the staff and a front row group of jet-setters and fashion doyennes. They always include Hebe Dorsey of the *Herald Tribune* and John Fairchild from *Women's Wear Daily*, two of the most powerful names in the trade. Around them are the buyers and bankers' wives, the mid-European aristocracy and Arab princesses, with a sprinkling of Left Bank intellectuals or performance artists, all fighting each other for the best seats. Yves St Laurent does things on the grandest scale and his famous cocktail party immediately after the press showing at the Hotel Intercontinental is always an extraordinary sight. The champagne flows and flows, but the food disappears like lightning as the handpicked guests – fashion editors, writers and private clients – abandon their usual composure to attack heaped silver platters of petits fours, hors d'oeuvres, éclairs and other delicious snacks. As a model, I never had a chance. In the five minutes it took me to climb into my jeans, the ravening hordes had devoured the lot. I made up for it with the champagne instead.

Rome's forte is visiting show biz. Valentino always throws a big party at his beautiful *palazzo* and if you keep your eyes on the guests instead of the paintings on the walls, it is possible to spot anyone from Frank Sinatra to Jackie Onassis. In the same week Eileen Ford, one of the top New York agents, has a famous lunch at her hotel. This is a key occasion as a barometer of model style. I remember one year sitting next to a young blonde girl called Patti Hanson, who was obviously trying to drop her sexy chubbiness for model emaciation. Six months later she had made it on to every glossy magazine cover and launched the voluptuous, sporty look of the early eighties.

Milan is the most dangerous place for model groupies. It always had the most backstage gigolos claiming that they were counts, princes or film producers and every evening I would find myself confronted in the hotel lobby by a gauntlet of hairy-chested, grappa-drinking Romeos with silver medallions and low-cut trousers. The trick, I discovered, was to dredge every final reserve of energy and take the initiative with a firm but gentle piece of abuse before the situation deteriorated. I received too many meaningless bunches of flowers and saw too many new girls pounced upon with a standard token of affection like a fake Rolex watch not to feel cynical and intolerant at the glib presumption behind the hollow gestures. I have never had any patience, either, with the bored man who has had one drink too many and has decided that anybody is his for the evening. If I get badly cornered, I pretend to doze off.

Practising techniques for escaping model groupies, with my great friend Brian Clarke in hot pursuit. A haughty look can work wonders.

Milan is by no means, however, the only city for groupies. They are a global network under whose auspices lurk celebrity or titled names, Casanovas with fat wallets and lonely men with empty hearts. Their lives seem to centre around chatting up unattached models and trying to get the phone number of every agent in town; in New York one of the agencies was even nicknamed the Pussy Farm because it held a soirée nearly every night of the week.

New York, on the other hand, is strong on money and hype. It has always been that way. Even in the thirties a Saks' shop-window mannequin became a society craze and could be seen having dinner and going to clubs, even making television appearances, with her maker, designer Lester Gaba. If there is a choice between a boring truth and an exciting lie, you can guess which one wins on that side of the Atlantic. The discovery of Iman, now one of the world's top black models, is a perfect example. She was originally persuaded to go to America by a photographer, Peter Beard, who had photographed her in Somalia and used her portrait on the invitation card to an exhibition of his work . By the time she arrived in New York, the hype and news coverage were immense. Beard had organized a full-scale international press conference at which he made himself out to be an intrepid explorer who had discovered a bush girl herding sheep. In fact, Iman is the daughter of a diplomat, a highly sophisticated and intelligent woman with a cosmopolitan upbringing and education. She played along for three months until her patience cracked at being treated, in her own words, like a piece of polished mahogany.

Quite honestly, a little fashion socializing goes more than a long way, especially since the worst gossip is often about the models. It is a very gay world too, and I have sometimes ended up feeling like a wallflower. There is always an end-of-the-week ball attended by everyone in town, but I often skipped it so I could get home in time for the weekend. If I found the time and energy to take the evening off – I spent most of them worrying about washing and setting my hair, getting to bed early ready for the onslaught of the next day or hurtling through last minute rehearsals or fittings – I always preferred relaxing over good food and a bottle of wine in the company of

Businessman, *grande dame*, designer and model: from left to right, Pierre Bergé, Diana Vreeland, Yves St Laurent and the author, standing on the steps of Yves's house.

other models who had also been working hard since seven in the morning. The best parties were always those with the people with whom I had shared the worst as well as the best moments. Yves's cocktail party was fun, but the lunch which followed his *haute couture* show was far more special. Every single person who had worked on the collection would sit down together , with Yves at the centre, to share the elation and excitement of the show. The only outsiders would be his mother and a few close friends.

The rapport with a designer is one of the most enjoyable parts of fashion socializing. The gossip columns only ever depict the designers as revered geniuses, bathing in oceans of champagne and the congratulatory kisses of high society. The reality is very different. Each show represents six months of extraordinarily hard and often lonely work with a nerve-racking run up to the final deadline. Designers like Yves, Karl Lagerfeld and Valentino, who do both *haute couture* and ready-to-wear, take on the pressure of a collection not just twice, but four times a year. They are all very different characters: Yves is very shy, Karl, by comparison, talks a mile a minute in a very enthusiastic way, and Valentino is the archetypal Italian charmer.

What counted most as a model was that he treated us with respect and was always interested in our suggestions on the way a dress felt – where a flower might be added, a neckline reshaped. Yves was always so considerate, allowing each of his models a moment of glory in one of the star evening dresses, giving us a special tea at the final fitting and presenting us all with bouquets after the show. In my day, we could also each buy one outfit at a specially reduced price – one year, I treated myself to a superb coat at a third of its true price. Now, quite rightly, he is saving everything for his museum.

The backstage world is a demanding one and it requires considerable acumen. Sometimes I felt it was perfect training to be a diplomat. Jealousy, bitchiness and backbiting would make life impossible in the pre-show pandemonium and there is very little of it around, although outsiders refuse to believe this. There are several essential social skills: the willingness to get on with everybody around you, the patience to get through the *grande passion* over a dress without losing your sanity, and the enjoyment of the company of women. In this sense, it is a little bit like going back to school – but with every nationality under the sun. There are relatively few French and Italian models, but the Swedes are always in evidence; their tall build, perfect bone structure and blonde hair make them popular everywhere. They are very down-to-earth about it all. Now, however, it is the Americans who seem to make the best showgirls.

Occasionally, it is hard to bite back a comment. Some girls are more interested in promoting themselves than the clothes. It was easy to forgive the friction between the in-house *cabine* girls because they were obviously desperate to seize their golden opportunity to climb out to fame. In my time, Yves had a beautiful model from Martinique who showed his clothes marvellously, but was universally and heartily disliked because she made such a terrible fuss every time someone else was being fitted for a dress. She seemed to have in mind a one-woman show. It is astonishing what some girls will do for the most glamorous dresses: once I even saw one model attack another with a bottle in a struggle over a show-stopping evening gown.

My own particular intolerance is for models who do not care about their work. The catwalk friends of whom I am most fond I also respect. As showgirls, Pat Cleveland and Iman are, to my mind, just the best. They

One of my favourite fashion shots, taken in Florence, with fashion stylist Michael Roberts playing the part of the sheikh.

Two of the world's best known modelling faces: Iman and Jerry Hall.

both have a wonderful smooth sense of movement that takes them prowling out along the catwalk like panthers. But more important than this, they are both terrific individualists. Jerry Hall has always said it was the black models whose style of showing taught her how to walk. Every time Pat goes out on the catwalk she gives everything to sell the dress. Crazy, sweet and slightly camp – she once asked Bailey if he thought airplanes had souls – she is adored by all the designers. Each season she develops a new style: one year, it may be Josephine Baker, the next, Dorothy Lamour. She even dangled from the ceiling as a Madonna for Thierry Mugler when she was four months pregnant.

Iman is special in a very different way. Proudly African in her bearing and witty with her tongue, she is one of the handful of girls who is able to do *haute couture*, ready-to-wear and photographic work. She has also done more than anyone to enhance the position of black models. Initially resented for successfully breaking in where others had failed, she has more recently been claimed as a representative by American black women and I have even seen her mobbed on the street by young admirers.

Perhaps my closest catwalk friend is Jerry Hall. We first met in Paris at 'Cover Girls', which was also her first show. When Kenzo introduced us I remember taking in only Jerry's height, the huge smile on her face and a headful of pink foam curlers. Ten minutes later she began to unwind streamers of shiny gold hair which fell practically to her knees and I knew immediately she would steal the show. Since then we have been through many backstage escapades and even more bottles of champagne together. Jerry's generosity, humour and perfectionism make her a great catwalk companion because she is constantly laughing at herself, stays relaxed at the worst moments of panic and can be as stubborn as a mule if I am feeling lazy about running through our moves in the last few minutes before a show.

By the morning of the show the designers are on a knife's edge. They work at flying speed right down to the finishing line, altering countless details and even changing the whole running order of the show to give it the right zip and spontaneity. I say hello when I arrive and then usually keep clear until I am ready to be checked in the first outfit. Otherwise it is too easy to pick up their nerves. The tension can give the right charge, but sometimes it is unbearable. In any case, there is always far too much to do.

First, and most important, is the strategy conference with the dresser. Behind every unruffled catwalk model, there is always a good dresser. English dressers are without any question the best; a clucky, motherly breed with endless supplies of tea and sympathy. In France and Italy I have always felt they are simply doing a job and in America you can hit real gum-chewing loudmouths. However you feel about your dresser, it is always crucial to keep her on your side. She has the means to wreak disaster. Many is the time I have stepped up on to the catwalk suppressing a grin as the girl in front walks on with her dress tucked into her pants, or, worse still, falls out of a low-cut dress that should have been pinned for safety by a cautious eye.

I always went over every item of clothing with my dresser, checking each zip and button, and arranging the shoes, accessories and tights for each outfit. With fifteen changes, each of which has to take place in thirty seconds, it is fatally easy to put on the wrong jacket with the wrong skirt or go out with a crucial zip undone unless everything is planned and you know exactly what lies ahead. If you spot the wrong size of shoe early enough in

the day, then there is always a chance for you to right this; if not, you end up hobbling on to the catwalk like an overgrown schoolgirl. Then we would run through all the possible shortcuts or trouble spots together: sometimes I would do up only half the buttons on a jacket to give me time to open them, or wear natural tights under coloured ones which would peel off quickly during a change. Most important of all, if the shoes were slippery, I knew to spit on the soles so that I would at least stay on my feet for my entrance.

Next came guerrilla warfare with the make-up artists and hairdressers. Each required a different technique. With make-up artists the golden rule was subtle supervision. In my young and innocent days I used to lie back with my eyes closed, but after waking up several times to find myself more like a monster taken out of the deep freeze than a brunette Marilyn Monroe, I always kept my contact lenses in and watched their every move. With hairdressers, Jerry and I always applied one basic principle – keep on the move and stay hidden until it is too late for the enemy to attack. This followed several pitched battles from which we had emerged severely scathed: Jerry with a forehead badly burnt by curling tongs and I with a scalping device of black electrical tape which had been strapped round my head by one of Claude Montana's hairdressers. There must be good reasons why stylists with honourable intentions towards a model's hair and body stay away from Paris, but I have never discovered them. After Warren Beatty's super-stud in *Shampoo*, the collections seemed to attract only young, randy incompetents. Maybe their worthier colleagues simply became unfairly tarred with the same brush in my mind.

Sometimes there would be a run-through to check the timing of the show with the soundtrack. Music can counterpoint clothes beautifully. I have done shows for Yves where the music has switched from Bizet to Puccini, then finished with the Velvet Underground. There have been occasional times when it was worse than nothing. One of the most frustrating shows I ever did involved showing beautiful clothes to the dirge-like strains of Mahler.

Whether or not there was a run-through, I always took a quick peek at the runway or stage to see what the surface was like. Some are as slippery as icy pavements and the masking tape put on the soles of the shoes to prevent their getting scratched makes walking even more dangerous. Then I check the turning space at the end – it can be circular or T-shaped – and look for anything else that might make me trip or tumble. Yves, for instance, used to have a huge chandelier hanging down in the centre of the stage and several times I became so carried away by the excitement of the audience that I bashed my head by doing one spin too many. During her very first show, for Halston, Iman stumbled against a mirror and did not return to the catwalk for three years. Once I saw a model who took off her glasses walk seductively into a wall and fall right off the stage. The real disaster, however, was that she could not stop crying, which shattered the mood of the show.

When it was time to change the backstage area would suddenly be mysteriously teeming with men. I have never given free peep shows, which meant keeping a close watch on the edges of a tent and double-checking the doors whenever there was a sudden burst of *argot*. Nevertheless, I could not sometimes avoid the feeling that most of the Parisian labour force were outside sharing gigantic orgasmic fantasies.

As the final countdown begins and the show music starts in the

Although the pose is very static, there is a wonderful sense of movement from the draping of the fabric, the flying hair and the glowing eyes. They are produced by a ring light, which began to be used a great deal in fashion photography a few years after this shot.

background, the adrenalin begins to run; once I did not even feel a pin in a turban draw blood until the dresser started gesticulating at the crimson ribbon running down my forehead. Champagne flattens the nerves, but only in the right quantities. The supply varies a lot. Yves gives no alcohol during work; most designers give just a few glasses; Thierry Mugler and Kenzo think in crates. I have always gone easy on the pre-show drinks since a close brush with disaster in my early days. Angelica Huston and I each consumed about half a bottle. Angelica was well able to withstand the effect, but I was weaving all over the place by the time we went out on the catwalk. I eventually missed my footing and dropped into the lap of a front-row fashion editor. Physically, no damage was done – I was so relaxed that I virtually bounced off the floor like India rubber – but it was professionally a mortifying experience. The editor worked for *Harpers and Queen*, I think. I know she was not amused.

The champagne still gives me other problems. I end up making last minute dashes through the backstage chaos of clothes racks, stage equipment and frantic assistants to try and find the bathroom, which is invariably miles away on the other side of the tent. Once I was so desperate that I had to use an empty champagne bottle, and as I stepped out before the front-row group sitting elegantly on their little gilt chairs, all I could feel was guilty dread that a thirsty Parisian workman might take an unsuspecting swig from the bottle.

Some people have other ways of getting high. It is terrifying to step out in front of ten thousand people. I realize I am lucky not to get stage fright – my poor sight helps a lot because it reduces the audience to a comforting blur – but I still think the cocaine girls are crazy. Sadly, there are an awful lot of them around and in no time at all they are moving on to the rush of the needle. It begins to show physically very quickly too.

I have trained myself instead to store the charge of the adrenalin and to lift myself, body and soul, on to the catwalk with it. From then on concentration takes over. All my senses are tuned: when to pause, how to turn at the end of the runway, where to stop for the photographers, whether to move on to leave the girl following me more space. But I rarely hear the music – without complete concentration on movement I find I make mistakes. It is a fast pace and the timing is tight. I have tripped on several occasions, but I have also discovered that if you go on as if nothing has happened you can trick the audience into doubting their own memory. There can be far worse disasters. One show I did was plunged into silent darkness when the power failed.

The elation of the audience helps. The gasps and exclamations in Europe are easier than the rapt attention of the Japanese. So, too, do the lights. Beyond the first four rows, I see only upturned faces in the dark. I focus on one friendly gaze at a time to strike a personal chord. But my feelings go entirely into displaying the clothes. I visualize and project whatever I know the designer wants – big shoulders, for instance, or a flowing line and I throw out looks which will reach the whole audience. As I move I am trying to suggest how the clothes can be worn; if I flutter, it is to make the organdie catch the light. In the end, it is that selling which counts. When the grand *finale* is over and the applause dies away, the buyers take off, the press move on and the socialites go home. At the end of the week only the orders remain. For me that is the greatest satisfaction: the knowledge that my performance has taken the inspiration of the designer to the eye of the customer.

Two beauty shots: the upper taken for Italian *Vogue* and the lower for British *Vogue*. This is a good example of how imaginative make-up and lighting can produce two completely different effects.

T R I C K S
O F   T H E
T R A D E

o many people seem to imagine that I wake up looking like a Hollywood heroine. Quite the contrary. Like every woman, apart from those few rare birds of natural beauty, I wake up feeling like a plain Jane – I need to know that the make-up artist and hairdresser have done everything they can before I feel like a cover-girl. In the same way, when I step out in the part of a beautiful woman I know I am fooling people. The difference for me is that as a model I have at my fingertips the tricks of the trade. As an insider, beauty holds no inaccessible mystique for me. I have watched the professionals developing the features and shape of a woman's face like the outlines of a photograph, and witnessed designers transforming body shape by a few adjustments to the way a dress is worn.

The art of modelling is simply that of illusion. Its tricks are those of the make-up artist and the hairdresser, the designer and the dresser, the photographer and the fashion editor – but also those of the businesswoman and performer. Every model has the tricks of the trade behind her when she steps out on to the catwalk, and I believe that everyone, woman or man, should have them hidden away too, to pull out whenever they need them.

The true professional's skilled control always hits exactly the right effect. As a highly paid model who was expected to be able to do her own face and hair, I quickly picked up the principles and techniques of the make-up artist and hairdresser so that I could pull off a rapid salvage job in case someone fell sick or I was confronted by a Medusa instead of an Esmeralda when I opened my eyes. Over the years I learned how to adapt my dressing room tricks to my own bathroom – and if I can do it with my short-sighted vision, then I believe anyone can. All it requires is patience, imagination and forethought about the effect you want.

I know that some women feel uneasy about spending any time creating a fantasy surface beauty. But as a performer who depends on the illusion for her livelihood, I realized long ago that time spent on yourself is not empty vanity or preening in the mirror. I believe everyone owes themselves a little time alone making themselves feel good every day. Bailey hit the nail on the head when he nicknamed it my therapy session. It is a sanctuary of quiet self-assessment and honesty at the beginning of the day, precious time to myself with the door closed on the cares of life. It is not the surface beauty but the art of making-up that I value; when friends stay with me in Hawaii, they are always astonished to see me diving head first into the swimming pool after I have spent half an hour putting on my make-up, but to me it makes no difference.

Nor is it simply a routine. It is a soothing ritual, almost a form of meditation, which leaves me alone, totaly relaxed with my own thoughts,

The professionals: Paul Gobel (left) and John Frieda (right). Time and time again their expertise has transformed me into a beautiful and glamorous cover-girl.

and takes me from a barefaced honesty to the morale I need to take on the world. In other cultures the link between cosmetics – outer make-up – and psychology – inner make-up – is far more fully recognized without the awkwardness of association with frivolous femininity. In southern India I watched the three-hour ritual leading up to the men's *katha kali*, a religious story-play for which the men painted their ink-black skins with ayurvedic pigments made from the bark of sacred trees, at each step abandoning part of their own physical and spiritual characteristics for those of a divine god. Recently, American researchers have discovered an interesting parallel: that everyday cosmetics can promote psychological well-being and speed recovery in the treatment of both physical and mental illness by encouraging optimism and greater self-esteem.

In the same way, time spent on making-up and dressing reflects care and respect for yourself, as well as helping with confidence and morale and giving others pleasure. I think the sense of guilt provoked in many post-feminist women by conscious thought about looking good is quite misplaced. Instead of abandoning pleasures and advantages unfortunately associated with sexual bondage, we should simply make sure we enjoy them in the right way. There is no need to invest a lot of money or attention in appearance, and there is no reason that it has to damage the rest of the world. There is no reason, either, why dressing up should have those associations with female strategy: we should encourage men to look their best rather than smother that urge in ourselves.

I start with a little honest self-scrutiny in the mirror. Fortunately, the shock is never as bad as it could be, because I have never been able to put on my make-up with my contact lenses in. Nevertheless, sometimes there is very definitely a shock. At these moments my mind turns to the favourite proverb of the make-up world: plain features make the best canvas. I often wonder what people would think if they could see models without their make-up on; I am rarely recognized without it. The right starting point for any make-up is a greaseless – but moist – surface. I wash my face with rosewater, which suits most dry to normal skins – astringent is better for oily skin – and, while the skin is still damp, apply a protective barrier of moisturizer to my face and neck. Then I turn to my *batterie de maquillage*. I

am a believer in having a few good essentials rather than heaps of fancy contraptions and my basic equipment consists of a double-sided mirror, eyelash curlers and clean make-up brushes for eyes, lips and face. For my hands I have nail clippers, an orange stick and nail file. Tweezers are my pocket-knife – I use them for all sorts of things from stray eyebrow hairs to splinters.

The same rule applies to cosmetics, and I keep a fairly small box of tricks. For my skin I need foundation, loose and pressed powder, blusher and shader; for my eyes mascara, a black pencil, transparent liquid make-up sealant, cake eye-liner and four or five eye shadows. Lips and nails require less: outlining lip pencil, gloss and lipstick, plus nail base, polish and remover. As a woman who grew up with the threat of the tidal wave, I think you should be able to go further than this and whittle your needs down to the single item you would grab for special occasions in the lifeboat. I am a sucker for lashes, so mine would be mascara. Iman says hers would be a black pencil which she can use for almost anything – contouring her face, or outlining her eyes and lips.

For three good reasons I tend to stick with the same products. Firstly, I will not allow myself to be brainwashed into wanting something just because it is new, and when I stop to ask myself whether a cosmetic I am about to buy is really so very different from what I already have, I usually end up slipping unobtrusively out of the shop empty-handed. Nor will I allow myself to be fooled by expensive packaging or sharp marketing. Many outsiders to the business do not seem to realize what is common knowledge within it: different brands of cosmetics are often made in the same factory and a new range often means more of the same in redesigned packaging. If you want to collect make-up jars, that is fine, but never be fooled into thinking you are paying for a better product. Finally I do not expect my face to act as a testing ground. If you do this, then do not complain about the eruptions of protest you will meet in the mirror as a result.

All models know the three products most likely to produce a reaction –

When I am doing my own make-up outside work, I like a combination of strong eye make-up, defined lips and natural skin showing all my freckles, with just the shine lightly powdered away.

moisturizer, foundation and mascara. I learned my lesson after Jacques
Clément, one of the top Paris make-up artists, quite innocently used a
highly acclaimed new product on me. The following day I woke up to find
my face covered with rough, red acne that stopped my income for three
weeks. I realized then how debilitating it is to have bad skin, and have never
since allowed anyone to attack me with new cosmetics which I have not first
tried out on the inside of my arm. Once I have found the right products
through safe and intelligent experimenting, then I stick with them. Even
though I believe in spending as little money as possible on cosmetics, I
throw away all bottles, tubes and sticks which have seen better days for the
same reason.

   After realism, decide on the illusion. The artful use of cosmetics can
produce any effect, from wholesome healthiness to sultry passion. You
simply have to evolve the one you want to create. Fashions and colours
come and go season by season, but my own make-up hardly ever changes.
Left to my own devices, I like to be a dark-eyed gypsy with natural skin and
freckles. For a show, however, a model must always use the colours and the
particular look designed for the show. I tend to be given the *femme fatale*
treatment with lots of heavy panstick foundation by make-up artists – in
fact Paul Gobel, a favourite of Bailey, who has done more than forty *Vogue*
covers, says the only way he can see me is lying languorously on a *chaise
longue* with a poison ring on my hand and wild cats purring round my feet.

   Make-up artists' styles are highly individual, ranging from the natural
look to high glamour. Paul Gobel, for instance, loves Hollywood glamour;
drawing on the ideas of fashion illustrators like Antonio and Tony
Viramontes, he uses as many as fifty carefully graduated colours on an eye.
On the other hand, Tyen, the Vietnamese *visagiste* based in Paris, always
creates very delicate faces. Often under contract to one cosmetics company
or name, as Tyen is to Dior and Jose Luis to Yves St Laurent, they
nevertheless all rely on theatrical tricks from their artistic training and use
less orthodox items. Heidi Morovetz, for example, Chanel's make-up artist,
who does much of the make-up for the editorial pages of French *Vogue*, has

for years darkened eyebrows with an ordinary pencil, which always leaves me musing about the theory that lead poisoning led to the decline and fall of Roman civilization.

Whoever the artist and whatever the effect, the principles always remain the same. The most important, but often overlooked, rule is to strike a balance. If you slap on everything from fluorescent cheeks and silver face highlights to scarlet, glossy lips and brightly coloured eyelids, you will end up as a clown or a drag queen. By keeping my skin natural, I can get away with a strong mouth and dark eyes; if, on the other hand, you like heavy foundation, hold back on the lids and lips. The other main guideline to the right balance is to build on good features. So many people talk only about their defects, instead of starting with their assets, and use supposedly clever disguises which simply draw attention to the points they were trying to hide.

Finally, always think about the light. When I have to wear photographic make-up outside the studio, I often feel quite conspicuous because it looks so dramatic and overdone; in the same way, colours which look good in a glossy magazine look hopelessly garish and hard away from bright white film lights. It is absolutely vital, therefore, to put on make-up in the right kind of light, either artificial or natural, and for your face to be evenly lit. Changes in season and climate can also alter the effect of natural light on make-up quite dramatically: the saturated colours suited to Hawaiian sunshine can look crazy on a grey day. My main problem is seasonal variation. Skin make-up in particular needs subtle adjustment and should be tested in daylight. I always try foundation and powder on my face and neck, never on my wrist or hand, which can differ by as much as three skin tones. I also keep light, medium and dark powder in stock and mix them during the year to match my skin colour.

When I set to work with my box of tricks, I start, as all make-up artists do, with a little foundation dabbed under the eyes, on the lids and around the lips. Many women use it as all-over camouflage, but it should not be treated this way. So often it makes people look older. I do not feel comfortable in it and I hardly ever wear it, even at work. However, it is an essential base for eye shadow and lipstick because it allows them to go on smoothly and stops them filling in the little lines around the eyes and mouth. If you do use foundation all over your face, make sure it does not look like a mask: it should be blended into the neck and applied with a damp sponge for a smooth even tone. Jerry Hall achieves a very natural daytime look by using nothing but a photographic panstick base, blending so carefully that the natural glow of her skin still comes through. If you are wearing an all-over base, undereye lighteners should be added on the top rather than underneath it.

For the summer, I like to leave my face fairly shiny, but in the winter I apply loose powder until I look like a geisha girl; then I brush it off and buff my face with little circular movements with a pad of cotton wool until my skin looks matt but translucent. Foundation wearers should press powder well into the skin and keep it as sheer as possible: old Hollywood tricksters used to sieve it through a silk stocking.

I have always admired the way women with ethnic skins have managed to look beautiful with very little help from the cosmetics industry. For so long there were only products for light skin, formulated around a red base containing titanium dioxide which tends to give a strange, slightly ashen or lilac effect on dark skins. The mica content of many eye shadows, too, can produce an unintended pearlized effect. Only in the last five years have things changed significantly. First, the industry recognized the lucrative potential of such a huge, untapped market by producing cosmetics specially formulated for dark skin. At the same time, black pride finally broke through the idea that only light skins are beautiful and encouraged women to enhance rather than disguise their darkness. Both Iman and Della Finch, one of the first black beauty editors in Britain, are adamant that foundation should be a shade darker than the natural tone. Despite the changes, it is still very difficult to match foundations perfectly to the wide range of colours in ethnic skins, and the best way of getting the right tone is to mix your own, or just wear well-buffed, loose – rather than pressed – powder which has no foundation in it.

Most models and professional make-up artists will advise you to steer clear of face contours. Away from the bright lights, blusher, shading and highlights tend to cheapen make-up and, unless applied skilfully, make a girl look like Irma La Douce. Iman believes the same is true for ethnic skin – that you are better off without the nose contouring and the other tricks that are often recommended. Away from work, I add only a touch of blusher after I have done my lips and eyes, often flattening it with a final coat of powder, and I never use any shader or highlighter. For a black and white photograph, however, I use brown shading with cream blusher powder over the top to make it stronger, and for a show I use very dramatic accents. If you really want to try your hand at contouring, remember that light coloured shading will make features like cheekbones more prominent while dark shading under the chin, on the bridge of the nose or on the temples will make them recede.

Next come the eyes. Always start with eye shadow. I believe in using eye make-up for emphasis rather than colour and stick to warm, neutral colours like rust, beige or dusky pink rather than bright or pastel shades for natural light. Both Jerry Hall and Iman share the same approach: Jerry likes brown and rust-coloured shadow and Iman sticks to earthy colours, as she calls them. You may want to be a bit more adventurous. Eye colours were very strident in the early seventies, then they calmed down and, by the early eighties, we had moved into the age of the clean-faced vegetarian girls – as Bailey calls them – wearing only foundation and mascara. But recently, slightly heavier make-up and the dark-eyed, smokey look have become popular again. Dark women are very lucky because they can go to town with glowing, rich colours – bronze, gold and copper, deep blue, plum or jade – which look far too painted on paler women.

Shadow should be blended in well and will last much longer if you apply it wet, but if you have dry skin or wrinkly eyelids then use cream eye shadow to avoid lines. Always blend the outer edges softly away with a face powder. Under bright artificial light, you can play with colour tricks: I bring on the blues and greens with a subtle hand and use gold, which gleams and catches the light. A pencil line, blue for black skin or beige for pale skin, worn like kohl above the lower lashes, opens up the eye, and a dot of gold highlighter above and below the pupil, or a smudged dark line around the eye, will also make it appear wider.

After the colour comes the line. Cake eyeliner wears better than pencil; I smudge it with a damp, stiff brush to avoid the hard, sixties look. Always use water and not your saliva unless you are camping in an infested swamp. Since Margaux Hemingway, eyebrows have been back with a vengeance and they are more often darkened than plucked. I have been doing this for years anyway, ever since my brows grew back scrappily, like a badly pruned hedge, after I had shaved them off for the kabuki show. Since I do not think eyebrow pencil ever looks natural, I brush on powdered shadow a couple of shades darker than my hair and then fix it with transparent make-up sealant. If you do use pencil, it must be with a deft hand: Paul Gobel uses feathery strokes in two or three shades – brows are never one colour – then brushes very lightly over the top with powdered eye shadow. Blondes can get a wonderfully glamorous effect by using a gold eye pencil. For those who do still pluck, go for character rather than a thin line, and keep the natural arch of the brow by tweezing only from the underneath, and always use a magnifying mirror to avoid a moth-eaten look.

Lashes are my greatest weakness. I love long, curly ones, so I use first an eyelash curler, then mascara; if you do not like curlers, you can try the old Parisian trick of bending your lashes round a heated teaspoon – not forgetting to test the heat of the spoon on your wrist first to avoid any nasty singeing incidents. Good mascara is a question of dedicated attention to detail: I always use a magnifying mirror to make sure I do not give myself a black eye, folding a tissue under the lower lashes so I do not end up with a computer print-out on the lower lid. A wand applicator is less likely to splash the mascara into your eyes. I powder a light coat of mascara to make a thick base and then build up lush coats over the top. Blondes should apply mascara to the tops of the lashes as well as the undersides, using an eyeliner brush to avoid any risk of a botched job, or have their lashes tinted with a waterproof dye to make sure they are black all the time. You can always tell real perfectionists because they pull out the little lash comb at the end to separate the lashes. False lashes are good for the elongated Sophia Loren effect. For this, buy them in a long strip so you can simply snip off the length you need and wear them just on the outer ends of the eyes, as all the professionals do. Be careful not to get the glue in your eyes.

I start on my lips before I have finished my mascara, not because I am a time and motion addict, but in order to get the right balance. While the first coat of mascara is drying, I outline my lips in pencil and then put on a dark lipstick, which I blot to a matt stain. Over the stain I apply a layer of powder, then a top coat of the colour I want with a brush. The extra time is well worth while; applied this way lipstick lasts for ages and gets rid of the hard line around the edge of the lips.

Lipstick is very much a matter of colouring and style, with a dash of fantasy. Dark lips are good for gypsies, but paler colours suit blondes. For a real killer effect, try a smudge of red or gold highlighter on the inside of a soft, rose-coloured lipstick. Gloss gives luscious, full lips and white teeth, but remember it leaves behind a lot of evidence on glasses and collars if you are being a naughty girl. For centuries black women tried to shrink their lips by wearing dark lipstick, but now they are enhancing the fullness with bright colours. If the pigmentation varies, it can give the strange impression of different colours on the top and bottom lip; to correct this use an undercoat of foundation and powder on the top lip or a special lip balancer. True reds are good if your teeth are slightly discoloured because they make the gums look pinker and the teeth whiter: gold or orange, on the other hand, highlight stained teeth.

Occasionally I like to balance my lips by a vampy splash of colour on my nails: either dark red to wave around at the end of pale winter fingers or bright pink to flash at the end of my toes for the summer. For a more natural look, I apply one or two coats of a nude-coloured polish topped with

a shiny transparent top coat, using a white nail pencil under the tips to make them look especially clean.

So far I have been at work for about thirty minutes. This may sound a long time, but the point is that the extra attention gives lasting finish. The only touching up I ever do, before going out at night for instance, is to dampen and repowder my face, and retouch my lipstick. While I am willing to spend hours to create a glamour girl who lasts for a split second in front of the camera or a brief promenade on the catwalk, my own make-up is designed to go anywhere without any further fussing until the end of the day. If it took up any more of my attention or mind, it would feel unhealthy.

The same goes for my hair: I like it to look good, but I put more time and effort into care than styling. This is in part because I am not very adventurous. Occasionally I look enviously at short hair and sometimes I have been tempted by it because I know it would also chop the list of potential tortures. But in my heart I know I want long hair to play with and hide behind. Anyway, I think I look like a chipmunk with short hair and I like to counterbalance my round face with a little height on top of my head.

Long hair is also very versatile for a model. When I first started, my natural waviness was always turned into a long, sleek mane in keeping with my exotic roles. The hairdressers would wash it, douse it in setting lotion, brush it till smooth, then twist it and curl it into a tight chignon which they fastened to my head with pins. When it had dried naturally they would simply brush it out into a long, shiny sheet.

The art then was simply to ring the changes. This I did as much with accessories as styles. My favourite have always been fresh flowers; in Hawaii, a hibiscus tucked behind the right ear means that you are taken and behind the left ear that you are free. Pacific girls like to keep their options open. The trick is to use a flower which lasts without water, a gardenia or an orchid, rather than a rose, which looks as if it has dropsy after a few hours.

The Italians, on the other hand, were constantly trying to give me turbans, which can be useful for covering dirty hair and other disasters: Jerry once had to wear one for a whole week after a hairdresser had branded her with a pair of tongs. On the whole, though, the harem touch is a bit too dramatic for everyday life. Sometimes I did go as far as the flamenco look, with combs and barettes fixed to sleek, off-centre coils and rolls of hair. If you do tie back your hair like this a lot, be careful not to pull it too tightly because it is very wearing on the hairline.

As I gradually became a glamour puss, I was overwhelmed by an urge for curls – not just a few little waves, but lots of big Rita Hayworth curls. My hair was too heavy for heated rollers so I became initiated into the art of tonging. This fitted well with my interest in spending as little time as possible on style: newly washed hair takes a curl almost instantly, and it will usually last until the next time you wash your hair. I did, however, discover that there are a few serious rules to tonging. Never attempt it on wet hair: the curl drops immediately and there is a risk of electrocution. Careless tonging can also cause serious burns, so practise for the first time with the electricity off. Finally, never give up half way. Legend has it that Mary Quant's lopsided cut came about because Vidal Sassoon was called away for a phone call half way through, but I would not try for the same effect with curls.

Once you have the knack, tonging is simple. Choose the right size, depending whether you want wild gypsy locks or rag doll ringlets, and, starting about two inches from the root where your hair is strongest and

least likely to be damaged by the heat, wrap the hair for each curl round the hot tube like a ribbon round a maypole, close the flap and hold for a few seconds. Then release, slide out the tongs and pin each curl to your head with a grip, so it holds the curl while it cools. If you use heated rollers, the felt-covered ones will prevent your hair from getting tangled – or try wrapping tissues around spiky curlers.

For years my hairdresser, John Frieda, strictly forbad me to have a perm. Perhaps I should hasten to add that John and I are good friends – when I first came to England, he was Leonard's assistant and since we got on instantly, I have stayed with him ever since. He is a marvellous hairdresser who cares above all about good personalized service. He was quite right to refuse me a perm because my hair was in such poor condition. To my mind,

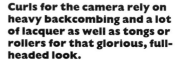

Curls for the camera rely on heavy backcombing and a lot of lacquer as well as tongs or rollers for that glorious, full-headed look.

the platonic hairdresser should be sympathetic but firm. He, or she, will always spend time talking and finding out exactly what you want before picking up a pair of scissors, but will also resist any nonsense and refuse to give you a style if it is going to turn you into a Martian or a witch. Since a good cut is the surest way of spending the minimum and getting the most out of your hair, make sure you choose the right person to do it. The technique of cutting ethnic hair is entirely different, so it is worth the trouble of finding one of the new specialist salons. If you cannot afford expensive salon prices, a model night where trainees cut, colour and perm under supervision is a good alternative. Shout for help and move fast if you think you have landed the class dunce. This holds true more generally too: if you do not feel relaxed with a hairdresser or your tastes change, never feel guilty about moving on.

On the other hand, a lot of disappointments come down to poor communication. Any changes should be the client's decision. Think whether you really want a style that has to be expertly set or blow-dried every time you wash your hair and explain to the hairdresser if you want a more natural look. Take along a reference picture – without unrealistically expecting to turn out looking like the goddess it shows – and never let the scissors start snipping until you are sure you know what you will be getting and like it.

After I had bullied John for many years, he relented when my hair was in good condition and gave me my perm, which has cut down daily care to a quick brush or comb. The life of a perm depends on the length of your hair: with long hair it may last for up to two years, but short hair may need re-perming with every cut. Over-perming old curls can lead to a frizz so they should always be cut out first. In the old days, a perm always meant a helmet-like, backcombed hairdo which went with a twin set, and the curls were very tight, made by tiny rollers. Now, however, perms are kinder to the hair and have been much improved chemically to give a very natural, light or wavy curl with plenty of movement. Nevertheless, I do not recommend home perms. Firstly, the effect is irreversible. Secondly, the strength of the perming lotion, the size of the curling rods, the tension and the timing must all be precisely judged to achieve exactly the right effect or there can be serious damage to the roots and hair shaft.

Chemical straightening, which is used by many black women, is basically perming in reverse. Nowadays, the curl is usually relaxed around large rollers rather than flattened. This can be expensive, since it has to be done about every six weeks by a good hairdresser; home treatments are available, but inadvisable because it takes a professional's judgment to determine the right strength of solution. The alternative is to buy straightening tongs – two large, flat pieces of metal which are far quicker to use than normal curling tongs because of their size. As ethnic women increasingly wear their hair natural or plaited, straightening is now on the wane. Plaiting is a very intricate, expensive process, but it does last up to four months and is said to promote faster hair growth as tension to hair brings blood to the scalp to nourish cells and causes them to reproduce.

Since the perm, my hair equipment has shrunk to a dual-voltage hair dryer with a diffuser – and a good mousse. This is undoubtedly the age of the mousse – and a relief after the lumps of stiff concrete produced by sugar water and lacquer. To add height, mousse should always be used on the roots and the hair then lifted away from the scalp by blow-drying; using it on the ends only adds extra weight which flattens the finished shape.

Setting lotion and wax also give fullness without an artificial, lacquered appearance, and, like mousse, can be used on wet or dry hair, or dampened and re-styled. Alternatively, simply bend your head forward from the neck as you are drying your hair, which also lifts the roots up and away from the head. Ringing the changes has also got much simpler: if I want to look special I simply pin up my hair in a tousled pile with three or four grips.

The final salon trick is colouring. Ever since I came back from Hawaii with a coppery tinge which the photographers all raved about because it broke up the solid mass of black hair, I have had lowlights added, for which the colour is subtly woven in and out of the hair every six months or so. This avoids drastic colour change or problems with regrowth. Low lights should always follow cutting to complement the shape of a style, and the tone should be one or two shades lighter than your natural hair colour, as if the lighter strands had simply caught the sun. Deep autumnal colours, like chestnut, are most flattering for black-haired women; blonde hair is best highlighted with tint to avoid the damage of peroxide-based bleaches. Jerry Hall does this herself with an aerosol spray, but you should only do this if you find a good product with conditioner. Products with a far lower peroxide content are now appearing, which makes hair colouring a much less risky process for women with straightened or permed hair.

Now comes the moment to dress. First, however, I always put on my perfume, in part because it can damage fabric and in part because I like to wear it all over, as part of my skin, so that I can enjoy the scent myself. Next I size myself up in the mirror. Clothes should always be worn with a detached eye for form and proportion, whatever your style, and there are lots of visual tricks to make the best of any body as a clothes hanger. I am not suggesting that you spend your life striking attitudes like a sculptor's model or mannequin, but an occasional session like this is a good idea to work out your good and bad points. It will also remind you of the importance of good posture. Simply stand in front of a full-length mirror, fully clothed, with a good friend whose opinion you can trust.

Always start with the good points. In my case, these are supposed to be my waist, shoulders and bust line. Joan Collins used to say that she could never work out what was so different about the way I dressed until I suggested that it was the sense of proportion I get by giving myself a waist. I always do this, and I think more women should, especially if they are broad on top. My shoulders are wide and strong – swimmer's shoulders – so I play them up, and my bust is small enough, despite all those teenage exercises, for me to get away with showing a little cleavage without looking blatantly provocative. My weak points are my wide face, short neck and, I think, my skinny ankles. I rarely wear short full skirts because of the ankles. I also have to be careful that I do not have so much leg on show that I look overbalanced, so I rarely wear high heels, which leave me towering over other people and make my legs look shapeless. To help with my neck and face, I try to wear sweaters which show the full length of the neck and I avoid choker-style necklaces, turtlenecks or shoulder pads which cut it visually.

If you do find clothes which particularly suit you then stick with them. Years ago, Tina Chow bought a pair of trousers from Kenzo at Jap and that cut is all she ever wears – she simply has them copied hundreds of times in every possible weight and colour of fabric. For good quality basics, like an evening skirt, it is worth going to the designer sales and paying the extra for a really well-made prototype.

There are a number of other model's and dresser's tricks which adapt well to the bedroom. Before a fashion shot, I experiment with clothes in different poses – some outfits look best with both hands, or just one hand, in the pocket, others with both arms by your side. When I buy new clothes, I always experiment to see how they move, how they look belted or loose, with both flat shoes and heels. I only ever wear full skirts with flat shoes, for example. With close-fitting clothes, remember to check that your pants do not show through. For shows, I used to always carry a pair of really old-fashioned, flesh-coloured, full – as opposed to bikini-cut – pants, which did not show through jersey extravaganzas as a line, unlike bikini pants. Another standard model strategy, also employed by Princess Diana, is to

Trying out a pose before a shot with stylist Peta Hunt.

One of the best things about location work is that you sometimes get the chance to do a bit of sightseeing. Here I am in Bali, photographing a temple.

wear thermal underwear on winter location work. This is how we manage to look summery in the park wearing a floaty dress, and to keep our smile without a heavy coat on a freezing winter's day. I always packed long johns and vests in every possible shape and size when I was going off on a trip, and still wear them a lot in winter to avoid heavy winter clothes.

The fashion business produces some of the most intrepid travellers I know. Bailey claims that on one trip to Kashmir for British *Vogue*, the fashion editor came prepared with masses of toilet rolls and even her own toilet seat. It may sound ludicrous, but having been faced by appalling sanitary conditions on so many trips myself, I sympathize. It is worth developing a little strategy when you are facing them so often. I keep packing down to a bare minimum, but make sure I always have the essentials for travelling at a moment's notice. The very first things I pack are photocopies of my passport (this solves endless problems if it gets lost or stolen), health insurance and current medical prescriptions, then my driving licence and travellers cheques – never cash. Spare contact lenses or glasses are also at the top of my list. Then I pack a standard medical kit: aspirin, anti-diarrhoea pills, mild antibiotics, Tampax, insect repellent, plasters, water purifying tablets to clean my contact lenses (I once suffered terrible conjunctivitis after using hotel water) and glucose tablets for sudden energy. For the tropics I add salt tablets, a mosquito net from a camping equipment store and a small bottle of duty-free whisky to use as an antiseptic and mouthwash.

If I am going on beach locations then I may take along iodine to slip into my suntan oil to tint me a good reddish brown on the first day. Most models lay down a first golden tint (very tanned skin looks dirty in photographs) on a sunbed, otherwise known as an Automatic Ageing Machine, a name given to it by the eminent American dermatologist Dr Albert Kligman. Used on a regular basis, sunbeds can have a seriously damaging effect on the skin and I would not use them for an all-year-round tan, but for work I will not risk sunburn. Some clients will charge for delayed time or simply refuse payment if a girl is looking like a boiled lobster.

The other occupational hazard of modelling is flying. Unfortunately, I hate it. This is mainly due to nerves, which I try to overcome by taking along all my lucky charms, my own music and lots of paperbacks, and then, once I have got on the plane, putting on my blinkers and going straight off to sleep. I break all the rules and do this with the help of a few glasses of champagne. I know dry atmosphere and pressure increase the dehydration but I still prefer that to sleeping tablets. I am also very wary of delayed or lost luggage and pack not only my valuables, but also essentials to take me through the first day. For comfort I always wear jeans with a T-shirt under a shirt, which I take off and hang up until we are about to land, and sneakers or sandals rather than shoes or boots, because of the way feet can sometimes swell up like puffballs. I never wear foundation or powder either, because it is so bad for skin in a dry atmosphere, but instead pack a face cloth and a small bottle of rosewater and moisturizer to dab on my face whenever my skin feels tight and dry. I pull out the face cloth just before landing and wrap it around a few cubes of ice from the cocktail bar to wipe over my face and wrists. This wakes me up and gets me through the terrible slog of customs and immigration.

When I am on location, I have a simple but strict code of conduct to ensure that I do not get sick or run into any trouble. I am very careful about

what I eat and drink, particularly in the tropics, and I avoid raw vegetables – eating only fruit I can peel – and never experiment with food from stalls or markets. I am equally strict with water: I never put ice in drinks, and always clean my teeth with proprietary mineral water. Nor can a model afford to invite trouble. I always find it extraordinary how many people leave their common sense and courtesy behind when travelling. Getting aggressive with hapless innocents who do not speak English is to be avoided at all costs, as is walking around in clothes which might be found provocative. I am also constantly amazed by people who forget to switch off the light, or even to lock their room, and are then surprised when they return to find it swarming with mosquitoes – or empty of valuables.

I suspect many people still believe in the stereotype of a model as a dumb girl who simply has to stand still and look good. Far from it. As modelling has turned into a maze of business and money complexities, the survivors usually speak two languages and are also smart financial cookies. A model is self-employed, relying on the service of an agent to find work for you and negotiate terms, but an agent can only help someone who is prepared to help herself. A lot always comes down to your own decisions and instinct about whether or not you want to change your image, work in another country or perhaps even disappear from the scene for a while. I suppose the most crucial such change for me was abandoning the limitations of my early seventies orientalism.

It is impossible to know what your working life span will be. An average career can span seven to possibly ten years, and in America, particularly, even longer. But as the wheel of fashion spins faster, the pressure for new faces gets greater and models get younger – perhaps as young as fourteen

Advertising people sometimes have funny ideas about how to sell a product. In this instance, believe it or not, I was modelling the shirt.

years old – the turnover of models is becoming faster. Someone like Jean Shrimpton simply could not exist today because no magazine is going to use a girl solidly for four years any more. It is no solution to change agencies to find work either; especially since the majority of agencies will not take back girls that have left them once. I have changed agents only twice – once in New York and once in Paris – but it was a good decision both times. I am lucky because I am a high fashion model and there will always be a market for their kind of clothes: you cannot model Yves St Laurent without sophistication.

A model who is a recognizable personality has to develop a particularly acute sense of marketing. Even today I have to think about striking the right balance between badly paid editorial jobs, which suit my image, and advertising or endorsement work, which brings in the money. Some fashion editors do not like using girls who become overexposed, but very few models now reach the point where they have to start thinking in terms of limiting their work. I only found the power to be choosy – and to stop sending out my composite card – well after I started working with Bailey. At one point, British *Vogue* told me about several letters from readers complaining that they were sick to death of the sight of me. We did try to vary things in a jokey way – once I even wore a blonde wig – but it did not really work. It is also important that people do not think you have become so choosy that you are not available for bookings. During the seventies, a false rumour got around that I would not work with anyone but Bailey and as a result I lost a lot of work.

In the end, of course, the most important tricks do not belong to any one trade. But modelling is a fast way to learn them. Since the art of modelling is that of illusion, you quickly realize how important it is never to fall for the illusion yourself. You also learn about rejection. To sell yourself can be a demoralizing and exhausting experience, and without a very resilient character, you can be drowned by the hurt of constant rejection or swamped by the hype of success at such an early age. When you have been passed over three or four times in favour of another model, or even unceremoniously dropped during an agency clear-out, it is hard not to feel insecure or become obsessive about whatever you think might be wrong with you.

Backstage, too, you can find cut-throat competition among models. Modelling has always been seen as a glamour profession and, in particular, a stepping stone to design and cinema – ever since Florenz Ziegfeld snapped up models for his follies in the thirties. The pressure has got much worse recently with the added financial and travel opportunities, and it is most severe of all for ethnic models since there is still far less photographic work for them in both America and England. When I was growing up, there were never any ethnic women in advertisements and there are still agencies who have only one or two token girls on their books. In a very few cases this may be due to the agency itself, but the real problem goes far deeper – to the continuing reluctance of advertising and editorial clients to change their attitudes and recognize ethnic markets. The drug abuse, too, is appalling. It has become far more severe as fashion has become a high-pressure industry; the heroin, cocaine and speed make their way into the dressing room not, as so many outsiders think, as pain-killers for starvation diets, but as safety valves for escape.

Success can also be difficult, although I refuse to allow it as a problem. It certainly provokes the worst jealousy; I cope by pretending that I simply have not heard hurtful remarks. It also provokes the worst hype; I deal with that by remembering that the applause and the fuss are never for me, but for the dress or photograph. I have discovered that these tricks have much wider applications. Never believe the hype or adoration. If you have been lucky, always pass it on.

There is one final art, and that is developing a fine sense of balance. Modelling is a tightrope between tears and laughter, the modesty necessary to keep your soul intact and the self-confidence you must develop to sell yourself as a beautiful woman, the will to survive and the good sense to remember how little it all really matters. To combine those is difficult. It needs the ability to confront the fact that the surface beauty on which your livelihood depends is really worth very little beyond that. When I confront myself in the mirror again at the end of the day to wash away the tricks, it is that barefaced honesty of mind and body that I always want to find.

A drawing by Tony Viramontes, one of the world's most famous fashion illustrators.

'Personality counts for at least fifty per cent of a model's potential.'

John Casablanca, president, *Elite Model* Management Corporation, International agency

'When a girl comes out of a model school, she usually has to unlearn everything she has been taught.'

Laraine Ashton, director, *Laraine Ashton IFM*, London agency

'A good agency will never take you on unless they are sure you are likely to succeed. They do not want to waste your time any more than they want to waste their own. Working only once a week is no good for a model and no good for her agent.'

José Fonseca, director, *Models One*, London agency

STARTING OUT

The right approach

Modelling is a demanding career which requires complete commitment and the will to succeed, a lot of hard work and stamina, the willingness to sacrifice your personal life for your work and the highest professional standards. Personality is not simply a question of projecting charisma and vivaciousness for the camera. The right attitude and interest in your work will always be one of the deciding factors in the choice of girl who gets the job: agencies' and photographers' most common complaint is that new models do not take their work seriously enough and have a sloppy attitude to the job. The right starting point is, therefore, the right approach – the realization that modelling is not easy money or glamour, that chance discovery and overnight success are both extremely rare and that everyone is working hard to help you look good only for a purpose – to sell a dress or a product. Never allow yourself to be persuaded by a talent scout unless you are sure it is the right job for you.

The basic physical requirements are height – you should be at least 5'8'' and preferably taller – with a good figure and posture, and clear skin and hair in good condition. The oldest starting age is now twenty-one due to the constant demand for new, young faces and the time you need to make it a career worth your while. You should not realistically go into modelling for less than a year because you need that time to make good the initial investment of time and expense to establish yourself.

Finding an agent

The addresses of agencies can be found in handbooks or even the telephone book. Always make sure they are members of the national association controlling professional practice: in England the A.M.A., in America the M.M.A. and in France the S.A.M. Agencies usually set aside several days a week to see girls, but you must make an appointment. Take along any photographs you have, but remember that it is the individual style, pleasantness and enthusiasm you show in the few minutes given to you that really count. Be completely honest about your qualifications and ambitions, so the agency can give you an honest assessment.

Always ask why you have been turned down if that is the case. Top agencies often have literally no room on their lists. Others may be dealing only in a type of look or work to which you are not suited: photographic models may specialize in editorial work, for which you need to be particularly tall and slim with a lot of personality; catalogue work, for which you should be easily identifiable by particular markets; or advertising and commercial work, for which a good smile and individual features, like legs or teeth, may overcome problems of height and age. Show models must be individualists who know how to move.

Never become despondent through rejection if you believe you have potential. Remember that agents are fallable and that many top models are not immediately recognized.

Tests, go-sees and castings

Once you have been accepted by an agency, they will invest their time, money and good name to help you. Since the agent is essentially the figurehead of a busy company, your dealings will be with your booker. Model bookers are guardian angels who, through their contacts and recommendations, can make or break their charges' reputations, since it is their responsibility to promote you for appointments and bookings. Formulate your style with their advice; never cut or colour your hair without consulting them for example. In test appointments, go-sees, or castings, it is always vital to look your best and to give everything since they are the few moments you have in which to make an impression. This has become doubly important now that they are recorded on video and kept for future reference.

Tests are your first appointments, arranged with photographers who may book you for a session of test shots. Photographers can afford to be choosey since they may be seeing ten girls a day and, because the photographs are also for their benefit, they are paying for the make-up artist, hairdresser and film. The model, however, pays for the prints. You should always keep doing test shots, even if you have started to find work, because they are an invaluable way of learning, developing your own style (always look at the contact sheets) and establishing contacts. They also give you a constantly changing portfolio: a model is only as good as her last shot. Do not despair if you are turned down a lot at first and the agency must arrange test shots with a photographer who charges.

Go-sees and castings are arranged with fashion editors, photographers and any other clients for possible bookings. They may be demoralizing as you will often be visiting ten studios or offices in a day and there is often no immediate feedback, but it is vital that you remain cheerful. At castings, which are organized by advertising agencies or clients, you can be up against fifty to a hundred girls and selling ability for the particular product or market is vital. For fashion and photography go-sees, image and individual style is more important since hidden potential tends to be more easily recognized. Never take it personally if you do not get a job.

Starting expenses

The initial financial outlay, in your first year, is largely to cover the printing costs of promotional material, but also for cosmetics and travel expenses. Since these will not be reimbursed, although they may be set against income for tax purposes, it is a good idea to have a reserve fund: at 1985–86 prices allow £600–700. Do not let anyone persuade you to pay an entrance fee to an agency or subscribe to model directories.

The composite card, a model's calling card, is usually first printed after three to four months of tests. These cards are redone every six months, with the test shots replaced by your best recent editorial or advertising work. The card gives details of height, colouring and measurement alongside a large photograph on one side, and on the other, three or four more varied pictures, often including a swimwear and evening clothes shot. Standard black-and-white cards cost about £150 per thousand.

The head sheet and agency book: general agency promotional material are a poster-size sheet printed with a reference head shot for each girl on the agency list, and a book with the photographs of each girl's composite card. Both are sent out annually worldwide to clients and photographers.

First jobs

You should keep in daily contact with your booker, in the morning and evening, to find out about future bookings and check arrangements for the following day. Bookings will often be provisional, but if another definite job comes for the same day your first client will be asked to confirm or cancel. Do not feel apprehensive about your first job; the client and photographer will do everything to help you. Simply concentrate on being professional, above all prepared for any eventuality. Make sure your booker has briefed you and given you the names of the photographer, hairdresser and make-up artist and it is always important to do a little preliminary research on the photographer's style or the product.

A booking lasts a minimum of two hours although the standard working day is 9 a.m. to 6 p.m., or eight hours. Do not expect long or regular breaks and be prepared to leave quickly at the end of the day, possibly without removing your make-up, so that you do not hold up other people. Always arrive on time with clean hair, nails and face, but without any make-up (unless you are told otherwise), carrying your own cosmetics and hair kit in case of emergencies. Do not wear any tight clothes which may leave flesh marks, check your outfits when you arrive and, if necessary, change into a towel or loose gown to remove strap marks. Be adaptable, but never do anything about which you feel unsure, like a topless shot or something dangerous and always feel you can phone your agent if you are worried.

For location jobs, whether it is a day trip up a Swiss alp or a longer outing to Bali, remember that amiability and adaptability are the name of the game. Warn the photographer if you are oversensitive to sun, cannot swim or ski. Do not complain and do not take advantage of expense account bills at a hotel. Finally, always avoid any unnecessary tension within the work team; this includes sexual entanglements.

The international network

To be successful today, you must work worldwide, for which you are dependent on the international network. Agents from Paris, Milan and New York come to scout for talent in London every two to three months, and if they take you on to their books and you begin to get jobs abroad your home agency will liaise and make the necessary arrangements. You need an agent for every country in which you work (a model may well have up to ten agents) and the necessary working papers – and visas, which should be

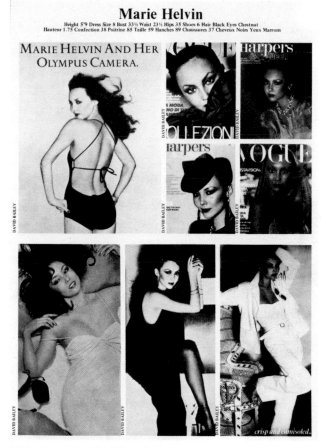

Marie Helvin

Height 5'9 Dress Size 8 Bust 33½ Waist 23½ Hips 35 Shoes 6 Hair Black Eyes Chestnut
Hauteur 1.75 Confection 38 Poitrine 85 Taille 59 Hanches 89 Chaussures 37 Cheveux Noirs Yeux Marrons

MARIE HELVIN AND HER OLYMPUS CAMERA.

This shows both sides of my last composite card.

arranged in liaison with the agent in the country where you will be working.

New York has been the mecca of modelling since the late seventies because the money there is so good. Paris is excellent for variety of work and prestige and Milan for editorial work which gives good photographic experience. London remains poorly paid, but is good for the chance to work with particular photographers and designers. There is plenty of work in Japan and the quality of tear sheets is improving, but recently the market has been flooded by European models.

Each country has different rules for payment of fees and work permits, and you must always be careful to observe the regulations: France, for example, levies a social security tax, and in Italy you must register with the police. Most countries impose a standard 20% agency commission. For Japan or the United States, you must have the correct visa in your passport, cleared for you by an agent in Tokyo or New York. Be very wary of signing contracts with Japanese agents, since many of them promise the air fare and accommodation without mentioning that everything must be reimbursed. Tokyo is one of the most expensive cities in the world and the commission is very high: your agent will clear 30% and a further 20% goes to income tax and resident's tax.

Fees

Models are technically self-employed and responsible for paying their own tax, social security and, in some cases, VAT. Once you begin to work, you should also find an accountant to look after your money and work out your tax alongside the possible relief benefits for which you are eligible, which may include cosmetics, magazines and clothes. All agencies have their own accounting service, but it is vital for you to have your own accountant as the agency will not deal with models' personal accounts.

The models who make big money are not, in general, the well-known faces because editorial rates are so low. To give a general idea of the range of fees, a new photographic model in London receives a daily rate of £35–100 for editorial work or £250 for advertising, and £150 for a show. By contrast, the American daily rate is $90–120 for editorial, $1,500–2,000 for advertising, and $100–150 an hour for show work. Your fee is supposed to be paid thirty days after the client has received an invoice, but it can often be two or three months as clients are notorious for paying late. This is nearly always the reason for delayed payment. The agency will provide an advance, usually at a commission fee of 5%. Cancellation fees vary, depending on the amount of notice given. The overtime rate is time-and-a-half between 6 p.m. and midnight, double-time on Sundays and individually negotiable after midnight. A few agencies work on a voucher system which generates a regular weekly income for the models and an element of security, but adds 7–10% to the standard agency commission.

BODY
PHILOSOPHY

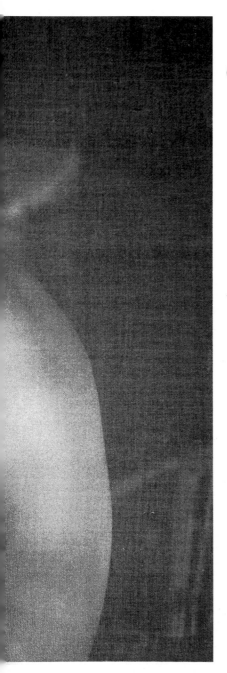

ody philosophy is simply internal style. Mine, like that of most people, has developed from childhood habits. I grew up thinking of good food as exotic fruit from the back garden and fish fresh from the sea, of exercise as the sensual thrill of running barefoot along a beach fringed with palm trees at dusk. Hawaii seemed magically poised between the ocean and the sky, and the sense of equilibrium I felt in the watery horizons, lush green land and scented air of the islands made me instinctively look for the same kind of balance in my own body. I never formalized this clearly in my mind until, as a model, I became more finely tuned to the needs of my body and began to notice that the condition of my skin and hair depended on a good diet, my energy on exercise and my inner calm on relaxation. Since then I have come to realize that my body philosophy is built around my childhood taste for doing things naturally and my instinctive feel for a balance between mind, body and spirit.

My style caters for the undisciplined spirit who relishes the good things of life as well as health, but I owe a great deal, too, to my father's vegetable juices, press-ups and vitamin pills. I could never stick to a healthy diet or exercise unless they were also a pleasure, and while I still stick to a largely meatless diet, do not imagine for a minute that I am a caricature who survives on bean curd and lentils. I like to hop between my favourite cuisines: Hawaiian-style snacks, tropical fruit and seafood, Japanese raw fish and *sushi*, American salads and sandwiches, garlicky Italian pasta dishes, Middle Eastern *mezze*, English soups and cheeses, Indian curries and samosas. The one sight I do hate is an overloaded plate. For me, style in food is always quality rather than quantity.

My father did manage to teach me to see food as fuel, as well as taste and texture, and to pay attention to the outward signs of what my body needed. Since suffering from morning migraines caused by low blood-sugar a few years ago, I now always have a large breakfast – toast, yoghurt and tea with either fruit juice and a boiled egg in summer, or cheese and toast or porridge, which I eat as Americans do, with butter and brown sugar, in winter. That usually carries me through the day, and I simply pick up a cheese sandwich, fresh fruit or some nuts when I feel hungry, but if I know I am going to be marooned in a sea of junk food or burning up a lot of energy, then I make myself a high-protein energy-shake (see page 155) to take along in a thermos flask or, for airplane journeys, pack fiddly natural snacks like pistachios or bananas, which will both fill me up and alleviate the boredom. A jar of peanut butter is another good stand-by.

A balanced diet is not, however, simply packing in a high dose of nutrients, but also the way that you prepare your food, to ensure the

People often envy models who work in the sun; and certainly seaside shots look very tantalizing with their long stretches of sandy beach, clear blue seas and skies and models seemingly relaxed and carefree, lapping up the sun. In reality, such shots can be very uncomfortable. There's both the heat factor, which makes the work very tiring, and the real danger of burning or of getting terrible strap marks which can stop you doing other work.

goodness is not destroyed along the way. Since I like the textures of raw or lightly steamed vegetables and poached or grilled chicken or fish, I find it easy to avoid the long cooking times and high temperatures which kill vitamins and other nutrients. Equally, I try to cut out the negatives – salt, caffeine, which make me very edgy, and alcoholic spirits – and to keep fats down to a minimum by avoiding all those cream cakes, oily fried foods and buttery sauces which drown out natural flavours. Then, building on that neutral base, I try to hit a balance within any day of about one-half fruit and vegetables, one-tenth protein, and unrefined carbohydrates making up most of the balance. Hidden with them are the naughty but nice things like Mars bars.

As a child the only meat I ate was a Big Mac while I was 'hanging ten' off a surfboard, and I have never tasted lamb, venison or offal. After nearly ten years of complete meatlessness I returned to eating chicken a few years ago, when I was famished on a flight to Hawaii, but I still find the thought of red meat obscene. Instead I get most of my protein from eggs, fish, cheese and nuts. I also use the vegetarian system which combines complementary proteins designed to produce meals with just as much protein as those of meat eaters. It combines grains with legumes, grains with milk products, or legumes with seeds in dishes like beans with rice and cheese, or beans with sesame or sunflower seeds. Water is also part of a balanced diet. I drink plenty, ten or twelve glasses a day, to flush away the toxins in the body; this helps the skin and kidneys, fluid retention and other infections. I also make sure it is bottled spring water, because running water exposed to the sun is said to absorb solar energy and to have special curative powers which can be passed on to the body. Finally, I give myself regular doses of live yoghurt, which is a natural antibiotic, and wheatgerm, which is full of vitamins and minerals, to fight stress and fatigue.

To balance all this wholesomeness, I have a vice – smoking – and the indulgences of any self-respecting food-lover. These range from the healthy sophistication of champagne and caviar to the nostalgic junk bliss of a plateful of barbecued chicken and chips swilled down by a pint or two of milk, or a tub of ice cream with a packet of oatmeal cookies. I would not want to ruin the greatest pleasures of life by guilt, so I simply save them up as a treat and then once in a while go for broke.

In an age when much shop-bought food is grown in hot-houses or kept in frozen storage, sprayed with insecticides and pesticides or adulterated by additives and preservatives, I think it is impossible to find all the nutrients we need for our skin, eyes, teeth, hair and nerves from our food alone, and so I take vitamin supplements every day. Since most of us work and play too hard we should not think in terms of avoiding deficiencies, but of building up optimum reserves to resist the knocks that inevitably come our way; research suggests that stress, smoking, alcohol and prescribed drugs, among other everyday habits, all lower natural vitamin levels. I often think in particular how much extra work and stress women have taken on in the last generation by trying to bring up children, hold down a job and run a household.

I am not trying to claim that vitamins are universal remedies, but I do think that to dismiss them as a faddish cult is to refuse good preventive medicine. I added to my father's vitamin wisdom in America, where as much thought is given to the way supplements are taken, and their hazards, as to the simple level of dosage. A New York nutritionist helped me to design a daily package suited to the needs of a working woman living in the high-pressure, unhealthy environment of city life, and introduced me to vitamins on a time-release formula, which allows absorption into the body at effective intervals. Many people waste the value of the vitamins they take by forgetting that the benefits depend on the body's capacity for absorption. Water-soluble vitamins, for example, are absorbed into the blood stream and lost within two or three hours without a time-release formula; oil-soluble vitamins, on the other hand, have a much longer life in the body and if used in excess can accumulate to dangerous levels. As an even more basic rule, vitamins should always be taken with food, never on an empty stomach, for proper absorption.

Rather than haphazardly working out your vitamin and mineral dosage alone, always seek the advice of a nutritionist, or a nutrition-oriented doctor, to work out your own programme. He or she will be able to advise you on the proper dosages you need. It is also important to try and understand the different effects of the vitamins you are taking. I take vitamin C, which is water-soluble, twice a day. It is probably the most familiar vitamin supplement thanks to Dr Linus Pauling's work on its ability to combat viral and bacterial infections like the common cold. A large dose is important for me, since every cigarette destroys 25mg; drinking and the Pill also reduce vitamin C levels, aspirin inhibits its absorption and at times of particular stress the body can need up to three times the normal amount.

My other vitamins – A, E and B-complex – I take once a day. Vitamin A, which is fat-soluble and can therefore produce toxic effects if taken in excess, is particularly good for the skin, hair and teeth – applied externally it

On a shoot all sorts of things are used as props. In this case it was the hairdresser Aldo Coppola who obligingly let me lie on top of him.

helps acne and impetigo – and its effect is boosted by vitamin E, which because of its benefits for cellular strength has in recent years become somewhat hyped in the beauty business as a youth vitamin that can retard the effects of ageing on skin. It does, however, have remarkable healing effects and is used medically for the external treatment of burns.

Vitamin B must be approached in a slightly different way because it is a complex group of vitamins and vitamin-like substances essential for the maintenance of nerves, eyes, digestion and skin. They are synergistic, in other words more potent taken in combination than separately. So, while each numbered type has particular applications – women are often advised to take B6 for pre-menstrual tension, B15 is said to be good for hangovers and B12 is especially important if you do not eat meat because there is very little in vegetable protein – it is always much better to take plenty of all of them as a vitamin B stress-complex tablet. The B-complex vitamins can also help if you have a tendency to anaemia or reactions to allergy-producing substances.

Every year there are new discoveries in the use of vitamins for treatment of specific problems. Iman once broke three ribs, her collarbone and her shoulder badly in a car accident, and was told by her doctor it would take up to five years to fully heal, but by following the advice of a specialist to drink a gallon of aloe juice daily and to take very large quantities of PABA (Para-aminobenzoic acid), a B-group vitamin, her ribs were mended within three weeks. Any such therapeutic use should only be under the supervision of a specialist, but it is sensible to boost your own intake if you are likely to have specific deficiencies through smoking, stress, drugs or illness which lower your natural body levels. If I am feeling particularly run down or I am convalescing, for example, I ask my doctor for a course of vitamin B12 injections, which I find have an almost instant recuperative effect. Women who take the Pill should add to their daily supplement time-released formula B12, which is particularly important to counteract the nervousness and depression felt by so many Pill-takers, chelated zinc, folic acid and vitamin B6 – American doctors also often prescribe this separately to help break up fat deposits on weight-reducing diets.

There is one mistaken use of vitamins, and that is as a substitute for food. Miracle diets and crash eating plans have always seemed to me far sillier than any so-called health fad. It is not only that I disapprove of unhealthy tortures for the sake of an idealized female form – whether a tightly laced corset for a sixteen-inch waist, a baby girls' bound feet or a starvation diet for sixties emaciation – or that I think many weight problems are in the mind. Far more basic than that, eating less for a short space of time and then returning to a 'normal' diet simply does not work and, when carried to extremes, dangerously imbalances the body.

Believe me, I am not saying this from the easy perspective of someone who has never had to diet, but from my own bitter experience of the pointless misery of see-saw diets. By modelling standards I was quite plump when I started. Although I never became as heavy again as I had been in my first few months in Japan, I was always having to shed a couple of pounds for a swimwear shot or a kilo for the Paris collections. Neither were there any special tricks. On an agency diet you simply eat less – or stop eating. I used to manage my temporary weight drop by living for a few days at a time on cottage cheese spiced up with herbs, curry powder, chopped fruit and raw vegetables, with an occasional stick of celery dipped in mayonnaise as a reward for good behaviour. If I needed to lose more, then I

kept to grilled chicken, or fish, and salad with yoghurt dressings for perhaps a week. I never allowed myself any fruit or fruit juices – people often forget how fattening natural sugar is. These are definitely good techniques for emergency action – doctors do say that eating only one food, even pasta, is a good way to lose weight – but do not expect the weight to stay off. After only one happy trip to a Paris restaurant my bony ribs always began to plump out again.

I stopped dieting as soon as I quit modelling the collections. For years I had felt unattractively thin and before I went home would always stuff myself for a week so that I would not feel I looked like an anorexic when I hit the Hawaiian beaches. Quite honestly, I feel horrified when I look at the pictures of me at my skinniest in *Trouble and Strife*, which tells the story of my own body shape over seven years. Photographers and designers may like flat, breastless wafers whose clothes hang off the body, but to my eye an emaciated woman is neither healthy nor alluring. Now, I have put on ten to fifteen pounds, which at first shocked a few photographers – including Bailey – and disqualified me from a lot of *haute couture* modelling, but I feel much more attractive than I did in my *Vogue* days, and that is what I think really counts.

There is only one way to lose weight and keep it off, and that is to retrain your eating patterns and to take more exercise. I firmly believe that if we eat only when hungry, resist the temptation to kill pangs of boredom or depression with food, and satisfy appetite with quality rather than quantity, eating at a civilized pace and thinking twice before bolting down second helpings, we should rarely be dieting. On the whole, I rely on moderation, but whenever my chipmunk cheeks get suspiciously round, I store my Mars bars in the freezer so they exhaust my jaws within a couple of bites.

Over the last five years, body shape has finally begun to acquire character, and I think there is real hope that the crash diet will become a relic of a bygone era. Models have gained ten pounds in weight and moved up two or three sizes to become tall, bosomy creatures with a lot more life; women who were once called fat are rightly being called voluptuous. This enlightenment occurred thanks to the American designers of the seventies, who looked realistically at body size in their home markets. Now, of course, the change has taken off everywhere and, since it reflects reality, I think it will survive other more passing looks. With a bit of luck, we may even get a few more curves.

As angular elegance has been traded in for muscled health, so fashionable body shape has become as much about exercise as diet. I am not a fitness freak, but I do think this is a step in the right direction. Our bodies, including their possibilities for movement, are extraordinary creations, and sedentary indoor life styles need the injection of exercise. Its benefits are too great to ignore. Of course it will never alone reduce weight, but it does diminish appetite, stimulate natural anti-depressant chemicals in the blood and reduce the impact of stress. In fact, the time and effort invested in exercise is best looked on as preventive medicine which shows returns not only in immediately increased energy, but also in alleviating health problems.

Nor is there any need to see exercise as an unpleasant form of self-punishment. All it takes is a little imagination to work out a way of exercising which you enjoy. Like many people, I detest formalized exercise and prefer not to follow the crowds. Jumping around to loud music in a class is my idea of hell on earth, and jogging on a cold, wet evening is not

One of my favourite poses – the easiest to hold. A fashion shot taken in Hawaii.

my idea of fun either. My style is definitely that of the free – some would say undisciplined – spirit. I like something which captures the exhilaration of running along a beach, or dolphin-diving into the ocean breakers, especially when I am feeling pent up and sluggish in the high-pressure concrete jungle.

I have worked out two different routines which catch that sense of release by making my heart race and my muscles stretch and which allow me to exercise wherever I am. One is for the working woman and the other for the mermaid. The working woman uses a cycling machine, the floor and a rebounder. The mermaid uses the ocean, a river or a swimming pool. Both combine aerobic exercise to condition the heart with stretching for muscle tone in the parts everyday activities do not reach, and develop flexibility and co-ordination as much as strength and endurance.

Swimming is one of the best forms of all-round exercise, and feels wonderfully sensuous when you can splash around naked or topless. My mermaid routine involves working hard at doing lengths. I follow those by four spot exercises, each of which I do twenty-five times. To achieve shapely arms and firmer pectoral muscles, pull yourself out of the water by holding on to a low diving board, with your arms on either side, and bounce in and out of the water, lifting your chin above the board. Then swim into the middle of the pool. Now, for a neat bum, bring your knees up to your chest and stretch your legs out straight, first in front of you and then behind you, folding your legs back up to your chest between each stretch and feeling the buttock muscles tighten up as you do so. Your arms will be working hard at the same time to keep you afloat. Take a breather, then follow up with two thigh exercises. The first one is the most strenuous. Stretch your legs as widely as you can, then scissor them diagonally, with first the right leg and then the left leg in front, treading water in between each one to regain your balance. You should feel the thigh muscles pulling against the water. Finally, support your arms and body on a lilo and, using only breaststroke legs, propel yourself forward like a lazy frog propped on a lily leaf. Suspiciously easy as these exercises may sound, they really do work wonders for flabby muscles.

My working woman exercises start with my cycling machine and some basic bouncing on the rebounder, to tone the muscles and condition the heart, stepping up the intake of oxygen through continuous movement. Rebounding is far less stressful than jogging and equally good conditioning for the body. I then do an exercise borrowed from the group developed for the Royal Canadian Air Force which I find excellent for the inside thighs: lying on my side, propped up on my elbow, with toes pointed, my body in a straight line and my muscles taut, I lift my top leg up to the ceiling and bring it down again – without allowing it to rest – twenty-five times. Then I roll over and repeat on the other side. Finally, I do press-ups, just as I used to with my sisters at the age of thirteen – twenty-five on the floor, levering on the knees not the feet, and twenty-five upright against the wall – to tone up my pectoral muscles.

Recently I have discovered the first work-out I really enjoy, a gym exercise class based on posture and free breathing, using the Alexander technique and Pilates' non-weight bearing method, as taught by Dreas Reyneke. Through his gifted coaching and individual attention Dreas has performed physical wonders for his pupils, many of whom are professional dancers – Anthony Dowell and Lynn Seymour to name only two – who come to him with injuries or other problems which require special attention they cannot find elsewhere. It was Dreas who achieved the famous transformation of actor Christopher Lambert's physique from that of a rather wan youth with a pronounced 'S' in his spine to the tree-swinging Tarzan of *Greystoke*. On several occasions he has also actually saved dancers from injury. Whenever I leave a class I am always aware of walking taller and straighter and I feel as though my spine has been literally elongated.

The Reyneke method is based on three fundamental principles. Firstly, Dreas works out no more than four people at a time, each at their own pace, with individually prescribed exercises. He regards the instructor's role not as imposing a set routine, but pinpointing the individual's needs – in fact, he introduced me to the notion of internal style. Secondly, Dreas teaches his pupils to maximize the out-breath rather than the in-breath, which shortens the back and tightens the thoracic area. Breathing out helps controlled movement by relaxing the torso and pulling the shoulders down, giving more control at the centre of gravity. I found this difficult to master at first, but the rule is simply to prepare for a movement on the in-breath, and move into action on the out-breath, just as boxers do when they punch

TEXT CONTINUED ON PAGE 144

I have always taken care to maintain a strong and healthy body. Not only because I feel most attractive when I'm fit, but also because for modelling you need to be firm and flexible. Many a time I have been required to get into and hold quite strenuous poses which, without regular exercise, I would have found impossible to do.

Although non-weight-bearing machines are an important part of Dreas' class, he has also developed exercises which can be done at home designed to cover three key areas:
1 The shoulders and shoulder joints, which determine the range of movement for the arms and neck.
2 The ribs (front and back).
3 The hip joints, where the span of movement of the legs is determined.

As Dreas says, 'Each pupil should strive to attain the maximum degree of freedom (without strain) in these three areas, because on that depends the placement of the head and the three curves of the spine – which in turn affect posture and freedom of breathing.'

The following exercises are among those Dreas considers most fitting for my body, but they were chosen by him for this chapter because they are of general value for all-round toning, strengthening and loosening of the muscles. Several of the exercises presuppose that you have a reasonably supple body. You should start very gently and stop if you feel a muscle is being over-strained.

In doing these exercises, your aim should be to free the joints *gradually*. Keep your movements within a free range, rather than so far beyond it that the body works under stress, which leads to eventual injury. Though I thought my own exercise programme kept me in pretty good shape, it took many classes before I felt I had sufficient stamina and agility to be able to tackle the exercises properly.

Stretches

For warming up and to improve posture.

A

B

A Hold on to a surface which is waist or chest height and tilt forward so your hands bear your weight. 'Walk on the spot', stepping through the heel, ball and toe of each foot. You should feel the stretch in the calf of your straightened leg as you do this. If you wear high heels often, this exercise helps prevent your calf muscles from becoming tight and foreshortened.

B Hold on to a surface which is waist or chest height and lunge forward, extending one leg straight behind you and bending the other leg, which bears your weight. This stretches your groin, thigh and calf muscles. Repeat five times on each leg alternately.

C Stand at arm's length from a surface at waist or chest height and bend forward so that your back is parallel to the floor. Make sure your back is poker-straight – any curve or hollow risks an injury to your back. Then, with both feet facing forward, either 'walk on the spot' again or lift your heels and rise on to the balls of your feet. Repeat six or eight times.

C

C

D1 Face a surface low enough for you to manage, extending your right leg, with the foot on the edge of the surface. Raise your left arm above your head and lunge forward, bending the leg supported by the table until you feel the stretch in your hip joints. Raising your arm as you lunge gives extra stretch. Repeat four times with your right leg half bent and then four times with your left.
2 Repeat the exercise, rising on to the ball of the foot which bears your weight before lunging. Keeping your shoulders down, try to feel that you are growing taller as you rise. Repeat four times.
3 Stand so that the table is to one side and extend your right leg sideways, placing the foot on the edge of the surface. Raise your left arm and lean towards the table until you feel the stretch in the groin and side of the torso. Again, be sure to keep your shoulders down. Repeat four times.

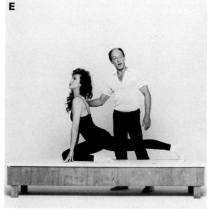

E Kneel on the floor, then move into a full lunge, putting your weight on to the front leg and stretching your other leg out behind you with the foot on 'half point'. Hold the position and push down gently until you feel the groin and hamstrings are well stretched. Repeat five times on alternate legs.

F Kneel on the floor with one arm above your head and one stretched out to the side. Move your weight to one side, while bending your torso and arms in the opposite direction. This exercise also firms the thighs. Repeat eight times in each direction.

G1 Put your weight on the haunch of one leg and stretch your other leg out to the side. Transfer your weight forward, leaning on your hands.
2 Staying in that position, point the foot down. Repeat eight times using alternate legs.

For the thighs

Not to be done by anyone with lower back problems.

Ha1 Kneel on the floor with your shoulders rounded, your stomach contracted and your head bent down. Raise one knee towards your bent head.
2 Straighten your leg back, lifting your head.
3 Flexing the foot, stretch your back leg away from you as if you wanted to push the wall away. Your weight should be on your supporting thigh rather than your hands, to prevent straining the small of the back. Bring the leg back to position '1' and repeat four times on alternate legs.

Hb This exercise is identical to the previous one, but after steps '1' '2' and '3' move your raised leg round to the side and, keeping your foot flexed and toes pointing downwards, hold the position for 4 counts. Then move it back to position '2', still pointing your foot, and finally return to position '1'. Repeat four to six times on alternate legs.

For the upper stomach

II Lie on your back, lift your head and upper back off the floor and clutch one knee to your chest pulling it as close as you can. Lift the leg stretched out in front of you a few inches off the floor.
2 Change legs, breathing out as you press each knee to your chest. Repeat twenty times slowly so you really feel your stomach muscles working, and then another twenty times quickly. Turn your head from side to side to prevent your neck from getting stiff, and if you like, rest your head on a large pillow to relieve any tension in your neck and upper back. Eventually you should be doing a hundred repetitions using alternate legs.

L1

L2

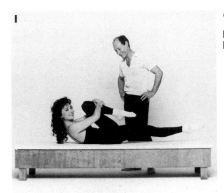

I

For the lower stomach

J Lie on your back, raise your upper back and rest your weight on your elbows. Keeping one leg stretched in front of you as in the previous exercise, bend the other leg up and 'scissor' it across the first, then straighten it and repeat on the other side. Be sure to keep your stomach pressed in towards your back. Repeat ten times using alternate legs.

Buttocks and inside thighs continued

L1 Lie on your back with your arms at your side. Bend one leg, raise your pelvis up off the floor

and begin to raise the outstretched leg.
2 Raise the outstretched leg towards the ceiling.
3 Lower your pelvis while lowering the leg. Repeat ten times using alternate legs.

Ma

Mb1

J

Mb2

Mb3

K1

K2

For the buttocks and inside thighs

Not to be done by anyone with lower back problems.

K1 Lie flat on your back with your arms at your side, your knees bent, and your feet placed twelve inches apart on the floor with your toes turned in. Raise your pelvis up off the floor.
2 Remaining in this position, move your feet away

from you, inch by inch. Be careful not to over-arch your back and try to keep your stomach pulled in towards your back.
3 Repeat the exercise with your feet turned out.

For the waist

Ma Lie on your back and then roll up on to one hip, twisting your arms and torso in the opposite direction. Roll back down on to your back. Repeat ten times on alternate sides.
   If in training, you will get the best results from this exercise having no support for your feet. But if you find this too difficult, you can use weights on your feet, wedge them under something like a bookcase or persuade someone else to hold them, as Dreas is holding mine.

Mb Half-sit and half-lie on one hip, balancing on your elbow, with your knees pulled up towards your stomach.
2 Stretch both legs to the side about 12 inches off the floor.
3 Scissor your top leg forward.
4 Take it back; return first to position '2' and then '1'. Repeat 5 times on each side.

N1

N2

For the inside thighs

N1 Half-sit and half-lie on one hip, balancing on your elbow. Keeping your hips perpendicular, cross your top leg over and raise your bottom leg off the floor as high as you can. Hold this position for six counts.
2 Try to stretch your bottom leg away from yourself and up towards the ceiling. If you are in the correct position, you will feel the stretch pulling all the way down the inside thigh. Strap two to three pound weights to your ankle to give you extra strength. Do this exercise ten times on each leg.

O1

O2

For the bust and torso

Each of these bust exercises should be held for six counts while breathing out.

O1 Sit in a chair and press the heels of your hands together hard, feeling the muscles of your breast contract.
2 Press down hard on your thighs.
3 Press your hands inwards against the outside of your thighs.
4 Push your hands upwards from underneath your thighs. This particular exercise also tones up the upper arms.

If you do these exercises naked in front of a mirror, you can see the muscles shaking as they contract.

O3

O4

Pa1

Pa2

Pc

For the arms

Do these exercises either sitting or standing with your back very straight, feet parallel and knees bent.

Pa1 Spread your arms straight out to the side like wings, with your fingers pointing downwards.
2 Make flying movements, keeping your arms very straight and flexing your wrists up and down. Repeat about twenty times.

Pb In position '2' of the last exercise, make six backward circles with your arms, flexing your wrists up and down. Bend them in to relax them and then make six forward circles. Repeat ten times.

Pc Turning your palms backwards and upwards, lean forward and hold the position for about six counts. Repeat ten times.

or tennis players when they serve – hence the famous Connors grunt. The third Reyneke principle is to exercise the whole body, and to use the dancer's method of working a muscle from contraction to maximum extension to give a long, supple shape rather than the bunchy, built-up body which comes from working muscles only at their centre points. Spot exercising tends to overdevelop certain parts of the body at the expense of weakening others, so Dreas will always counterbalance exercises. One for the stomach, in which the spine is curved, will be followed by one to straighten and strengthen the upper back. Otherwise there is a risk that the back will become hunched.

Although I was fairly fit before, Dreas's exercises (see preceding pages) have made me a great deal more supple and I have now even given up some of my working woman routine. As my posture has improved, I have also become far more aware of the damage done by badly designed or poorly fitted fashion shoes so I now wear flat pumps and go barefoot as much as possible. Very high heels are terrible and should be worn as little as possible.

Rest and relaxation are the natural balance to exercise and just as important to the body and mind. Sleep is the well of energy on which we constantly draw in waking hours. I also build regular days or evenings – and sometimes whole weekends – of relaxation into my life to allow the responsibility and cares of life to drop away. At least once a week I wake naturally, without a clock, and I spend my time quietly reading or mulling over recent events and my thoughts in peace. Stress may be caused by life style, emotional tangles, work or temperament, but it can also be linked to muscular fatigue, static tension from maintaining certain positions – like sitting down – for long periods, and mental fatigue. Whatever the cause, it is not simply in the mind. It causes physical tension which can trigger damaging nervous disorders or illness. I have experienced this myself and now make a conscious effort to combat and disperse stress.

I prefer to go beyond rearguard action. You are what you think as much as what you eat or physically build yourself into. Positive thinking combats anxiety; brooding on negative thoughts is just not healthy. Stillness and peace will be felt by your body as much as they show on your face. Many people are a little sceptical about alternative medicine and its methods, but if it gives positive results, relieves pain or discomfort and makes you feel better, then you should not dismiss it. It can work alongside, not against, traditional medicine. Meditation, yoga or massage can all help, and so, too, can visualization technique or body imagery, which is the basis of spiritualist healing. I was once told that whenever I felt swamped by problems I should imagine myself surrounded by a cloak of deep blue, the colour of purity. At other times, I take a more worldly approach; I watch television, have a couple of glasses of wine and climb the stairs for an early night, thinking of Scarlett O'Hara's motto, 'Tomorrow is another day.'

I only began to include my body surfaces – skin, hair and nails – in my general body philosophy when I saw their reactions to solid layers of panstick, lacquer and varnish: after a long hard collections week, my skin and hair would become as drab and lifeless as I felt. Then I finally began to treat them as breathing, growing surfaces. Until then I had never thought of giving them protection and nourishment. My hair was usually as stiff as a nylon wig from sea salt, and a loyal friend would help me attack it with an iron every morning before school to give me the sixties Shrimpton look. In fact, when my mother offered me up to Vidal Sassoon at a Honolulu cutting

SKIN

DRY SKIN

Dry skin is sensitive skin. It burns, peels, flakes or chaps very easily. It is prone to broken capillaries, freckles and fine lines, and needs constant moisturizing to prevent ageing. Black skin can be plagued by extreme dryness when subjected to cold, drying climates.

Care Avoid alcohol-based skin products and use instead a gentle cleanser and toner, such as rosewater. Moisturize well, paying particular attention to the skin surrounding the eyes. If you wear foundation, choose an oil-based one.

NORMAL SKIN

Normal skin is smooth, supple and well-balanced, with small pores and few blemishes or lines. It retains moisture and elasticity and tans slowly.

Care Cleanse and tone every day and use a moisturizer.

TYPES

OILY SKIN

Oily skin tends to be sallow and shiny, owing to an excess of sebum. It is prone to blemishes, enlarged pores and blackheads, and tans easily.

Care Cleanse with a detergent-free soap and lukewarm water (hot water stimulates the oil-producing sebaceous glands). Keep your hands and hair away from your face, sleep with your hair off your face and use masks frequently to control the oil. Never squeeze blackheads (this can scar and discolour, especially black skin). Use an astringent and an oil-absorbing moisturizer. If you wear foundation, make sure it is water-based.

COMBINATION SKIN

Combination skin is probably the most common type in the world. It is characterized by a T-shaped oily zone spanning the forehead, nose and chin, with dry areas around the eyes, cheeks and throat.

Care Wash the face with a mild soap or alcohol-free cleanser. Moisturize the dry areas regularly with a water-based product and use an alcohol-based astringent on oily areas.

These two pictures were taken in Morocco for British *Vogue*. Bailey had chosen a location that was within sight and smell of a refuse dump. My calm expression belies my utter disgust.

demonstration, he took one look and cut the whole lot off. I do not blame him.

The wrong starting point for skin and hair care is to rush out and buy a lot of expensive cosmetics. The right starting point is to work out your skin and hair type. This is quite easy to do yourself but, if you prefer, you can also have your skin analyzed by a trained consultant in a department store. The next step is to think of inner nourishment, and to feed your skin and hair naturally, from within. Both vitamin A and vitamin E are helpful to dry, flaking skin, while vitamin C helps to reduce sores and ulcers. Proteins are particularly important for strong, healthy hair.

The same ingredients are important in skin and hair cosmetics. I make a lot of my own, partly because I do not believe in spending a lot of money on them, but also because I like to know that everything I put on my face is as pure as possible. Using only a few ingredients – especially natural oils like hazelnut, apricot kernel, almond, wheatgerm, primrose and vitamin E – I have devised nearly everything I need for everyday use. I make my own rosewater, eye make-up remover pads, face and hair treatments and a rich vitamin cream which I use for nearly all nourishing (for the recipes, see page 155). Though I buy soap and moisturizers, shampoos and sun screens, I steer clear of any with harsh detergents and perfumes, looking for cheap, simple products which are acid-balanced and rich in natural oils. If any product gives me a burning or itching feeling when I use it on my face, I wash it off immediately with tepid water. In particular, I avoid mineral oils, like baby oil, which the skin cannot absorb; they produce all sorts of reactions, especially puffiness around the eyes. Equally, I never use any eye drops other than those with a homeopathic camomile base and prefer salt or baking soda as a less harsh alternative to smokers' toothpaste.

There are three golden rules in my skin care: keep it simple, go for moisture and do not think of the jaw line as a great divide. There is also one warning: beware the clogged pore. As a child I simply used to wash my face with soap and water and I have stuck to my guns ever since, despite the dire warnings of the skin experts, because my skin does not feel completely clean without it. Now the wheel has turned full circle and with the formulation of non-alkaline soaps which are water-soluble versions of cleansing creams, I have orthodoxy on my side again.

I am also scrupulous about washing off my make-up at the end of the day, whatever the weight of my eyelids and however passionate the moment. If I do not, then I know my skin will respond with pimples, large pores or sallow colouring. I remove my eye make-up first with apricot kernel oil remover pads then I slide off the panstick by massaging in a natural oil. Finally I wash with soap, rinsing up to twenty times with clean water to make sure all the oil is removed. As I have got older and my skin has become dryer, I have started to use soap only at the end of the day and to massage in oil first even if I am not wearing make-up. I did this initially to combat the drying effects of winter central heating, but now do it almost the whole year round.

In the mornings, I simply clean with rosewater. If I am feeling like death warmed up, then I start very gently the Japanese way, refreshing my skin with a face cloth that has been either wrapped around ice cubes, or soaked in rosewater and chilled overnight in the fridge in a plastic bag. If there is snow on the ground try a warm towel. I pat my face very gently – be particularly careful if your skin has a tendency to broken veins – until it feels wide awake. If a spot rears its ugly head at this stage, as it invariably does for me the day before a big job, I dab on a little natural yoghurt or a fast-acting prescription cream which usually takes effect by the following morning. Never simply camouflage a spot with make-up; it will pay you back by getting worse.

Cleansing of any type should always be followed by moisturizing, particularly during the day, to act as a protective barrier against the elements which dehydrate skin and make it leathery. Light-weight moisturizers with an oil-in-water base become even more essential as you grow older, for throat and neck as well as face. Since damp skin is always more receptive to moisturizer, I smooth it on to my face and neck while they are still quite wet. If you have very dry skin, you can also seal in the moisturizer by applying it before washing; Iman does this and finds that she can then do without moisturizer afterwards. Some people settle down with the same product – Elizabeth Taylor is said to have used the same cheap hand lotion everywhere, including her face, for twenty years – but I find I am constantly having to vary mine according to the climate and season. In winter, I also like a humidifier or bowl of water near the radiator to stop my face skin feeling uncomfortably tight from the central heating. Ethnic skins, which are really designed for moist tropical heat, often need extra moisture.

At night, I think my skin should breathe fresh air if possible. I have never been convinced by arguments in favour of covering yourself with night creams and only if my skin is particularly dry do I massage in my rich vitamin cream while the skin is still damp, blotting with tissue so that there is just a very thin film left on the surface. I use the same cream sparingly around my eyes, carefully removing any excess. It is also worth thinking about sleeping posture, preferably on your back with your head propped up by extra pillows, which will be far more helpful to dark rings under your eyes than magical creams.

After a hard week at work, I like to give my face a special treatment. For this, I use a scrub cleanser (or exfoliator) which is applied to wet skin and sloughs off dead skin cells and toxins. This clears flaky, mottled and rough skin, improves skin colour and texture, and removes whiteheads and blackheads. If you find this type of cleansing too drying, try one with a cream base or mix in a little moisturizer first in the palm of your hand. The same trick can be used with the clay masks which draw out oil and dirt. Always moisturize afterwards; I like to use a peeling mask, which locks in the moisture and lubricates the skin.

I have also worked out my own deep-cleansing facial steam bath, which uses camomile-infused steam (see page 155). If you do not have a face steamer, use a large cooking pot instead, covering your head with a towel to enclose the steam and bringing your face close enough to the water to feel the heat without a burning sensation. Steaming is a good safeguard against whiteheads and blackheads, which can be especially difficult to spot on ethnic skins. After steaming, I massage in vitamin E oil while the skin is still damp.

There are many other ways to feed your face. I have always liked using natural skin foods, and since my skin is dry I choose those rich in natural oils. As a child helping my mother in the kitchen I would rub the inside of the avocado skin or the zest of orange into my face because it made me feel grown up. Now I do the same when I am cooking, but for a better reason: avocado is full of vitamin E and orange zest contains vitamin A. I have known models who use everything from peaches and cucumbers to carrots, and others who wash their faces with yoghurt. My favourite is egg

Relaxing: finding the balance on a quiet, secluded beach in Australia.

mayonnaise, which washes off very well with hot water after ten or fifteen minutes. If you are buying a mask, choose high protein and oil content for dry skin, and oil-absorbent ingredients like kaolin, talc or oatmeal for greasy skin. Many people also forget that with a combination skin different masks should be used where appropriate.

The English fondness for soaking in lukewarm, dirty bath water has always struck me as a very strange habit, especially since my time in Japan, land of communal bath wisdom. Too much bathing makes me dry and wrinkly so I treat the rest of my body just as I do my face, splashing over rosewater or *eau-de-cologne* in the morning and using soap and water in the evening, staying in the bath just long enough to allow the steam to seep into my skin, then massaging in plenty of vitamin cream while I am still damp. Sometimes I use oatmeal to scrub myself in the bath, which sloughs off flakiness without sacrificing the moisture. Since I like my legs to feel as smooth as a baby's every day and do not like the spiky regrowth necessary for waxing, I shave my legs using an inexpensive lotion rather than soap or foam to avoid nicking, and then apply plenty of vitamin cream. For a manicure, I file my nails before the bath, soak my fingers in warm oil and then, after they are dry, push back the cuticles with an orange stick and cuticle cream. Polish often gives me an allergic reaction, so I usually stick to a buffer, which gives a healthy shine but also allows the nails to breathe. If I am wearing polish, I always use a colourless nail base first, which both protects the nails from the polish and also prevents staining from cigarettes.

Every few weeks I have special sessions for trouble spots – elbows, hands, knees and, when I am sitting around a lot, my bottom, giving all of them a good rub with a natural bristle brush to stimulate the circulation and then applying cream, or sometimes a pure vegetable oil. There are also some vegetable margarines enriched with vitamins and other skin nutrients which I have found excellent as body food. In the old days I would horrify Bailey with my Minnie Mouse routine the night before I was modelling close-ups of my hands or feet, by smothering them in cream and then donning cotton socks or gloves before climbing into bed. Not very seductive, but, as I used to tell him, a woman has to look after her assets.

The same holds true for tanning. My sisters and I always thought it a huge joke that anyone would cover themselves with shiny grease as if they were going to be fried for brunch, but now I, too, have become a tourist, who has to suffer the indignity of protecting herself when she goes home, much to the scorn of the old-timers. Many people imagine that as an island girl I probably cover myself in coconut oil, but I would not dream of it – and neither would you if you saw what it does to swimming pool drains and then thought about our old friend, the clogged pore. In fact, I think a good sunscreen is well worth the expense. Although tanning itself is a natural form of skin protection, ultraviolet light can produce cumulative and irreversible damage, decreasing the skin's elasticity, destroying its ability to hold moisture and increasing the number and depth of wrinkles.

Leslie Kenton, the health and beauty writer whose work I most admire, explained to me how a changed understanding of the ageing effects of ultraviolet rays has put sunscreen chemistry on the path to painless tanning while also protecting against ageing. Sun products now filter not only the short UVB rays which have always been known to burn and damage surface cells, but also the longer UVA rays, once thought to be harmless but now known to cause the greatest ageing damage because they penetrate so deeply, damaging connective tissue and collagen fibres. Some products

We were in Haiti for French *Vogue* at the same time as a Voodoo festival. Every night the festivities continued and we were all very short of sleep. I remember having real problems staying awake for this shot.

HAIR
TYPES

Dry hair results from a lack of natural oils from the sebaceous glands, which usually condition the hair. The longer your hair is, the more likely it is to be dry, because the ends are further away from the scalp. Dry hair is especially a problem for black women, as they have fewer and less active sebaceous glands in their scalp and their hair is frequently subjected to the dessicating effects of chemical processing.

Wash your hair no more than once a week unless your hair is very dull from dirty air, and use a mild cream shampoo.

Condition every time you wash, massaging the conditioner well into your scalp, and give extra treatments every few weeks. Pomades, oils and conditioners can also be applied to dry hair.

Avoid hairdryers which will lead to the loss of any more oils.

Dandruff, scurf or flaky skin particles can affect oily or dry hair. This condition may be improved by milder shampoos, an improved diet or head massage which encourages the supply of nutrients to hair through the network of blood capillaries under the scalp. Always follow the instructions for dandruff shampoos carefully or they can be ineffective. Try rinsing with an antiseptic solution diluted with water to half its strength after conditioning your hair. If dandruff is severe you should consult a trichologist; it may be caused by a specific disorder like impetigo which needs special treatment and which will affect the skin if left untreated.

OILY HAIR

Oily hair, with excess grease, is caused when over-active sebaceous glands produce too much sebum. Fine hair is especially prone to oiliness; thick, coarser hair tends to soak up excess oil.

Wash oily hair as often as necessary, but always use a mild shampoo, preferably one free of detergent and perfume. If you wash your hair every day, then make do with just one lather.

Condition only the ends of the hair. Never apply directly to your scalp.

Avoid vigorous brushing, which stimulates the oil-producing sebaceous glands, and heated hair devices, which can cause further oiliness because the heat activates the sebaceous glands.

incorporate anti-wrinkle and hydrating agents, others are pre-skin milks which encourage the synthesis of new melanin and help produce a rich tan in only four to five days instead of nine to ten days. I look for one which also contains PABA (Para-aminobenzoic acid), the B-complex vitamin which has a remarkable natural ability to protect skin cells from genetic change.

Now, when I go home to Hawaii, I put on my war paint before going out in the midday sun. I use a flesh-coloured sunblock on my forehead and nose – or for work on my whole face (occasionally leaving the cheeks bare for a nice glow) – and a colourless sunblock on my shoulders, bust-line and the tops of my feet, with a high protection factor sunscreen on the rest of my body. After I have acclimatized myself in the first few days, I scale down to an oil-in-water emulsion, which I am always careful to re-apply after swimming, even when it is supposed to be water-resistant. For sunburn, we always use the juice of the fleshy, cactus-like *Aloe vera* leaf in Hawaii, squeezing it directly on to the burnt skin. It is often possible to find the plants here in garden shops – otherwise, try a paste made from baking soda or, if you are as pink as a Virginia ham all over, soak the whole body in a cool bath with a few teaspoons of baking soda added to the water.

Watch out for unexpected photosensitizers, too, which produce badly pigmented, muddy patches that are difficult to eradicate. These include essential oils like bergamot, which is used in perfumes and sunscreens, and everyday drugs like the contraceptive Pill. Always ask your doctor about possible reactions if you are going to have prolonged exposure to the sun in combination with any form of prescribed drug; a few years ago I was turned into a patchy giraffe by an anti-fungal cream. The chemicals in swimming pool water can also do strange things, like turning blonde hair green – so it is worth the effort of rinsing it out, or wearing a special gel to protect your hair when you are sunbathing.

That frizzy mop which once hung off my head as a stiff, salt-encrusted mass later became my trade mark. When people ask me if I have always had such naturally beautiful hair, I smile inside and think of Vidal Sassoon's face all those years ago. The transformation was a long time in the making and certainly did not come because my hair led a gentler life. Quite the opposite. The damage to models' locks is always such that they have to spend a lot of time and effort to keep it in good condition. Imagine the traumatic effect of a collections week with every strand of hair teased, backcombed and tonged, then doused with sugar water or lacquer till my scalp was crying out for mercy, not just once but ten times a day. I always made the hairdressers agree to comb out their creations themselves, but that still left me conditioning and washing my hair every evening and spending hours in salons having professional treatments.

It is hard to inflict as much damage with everyday perms and tints or the occasional use of heated rollers or tongs, but all hair takes a beating – even the elements strip hair of its natural oils and shine – and needs careful washing and conditioning. Provided you use a mild, detergent-free shampoo, condition hair well afterwards and use products formulated for your type of hair and frequency of use, it is perfectly all right to wash your hair as often as you like. However, the good effects of a shampoo definitely do seem to lessen with use, for whatever reason, and most professionals advise that you change or alternate your shampoo every few months. If your hair is finely plaited, you may find it easier to wash it with a fine-toothed comb or toothbrush. Whenever possible let your hair dry naturally, because it is the kindest way, but if you must use a dryer, keep it on the

RECIPES

Daily vitamin supplement

1 Never follow someone else's vitamin programme. Work out your own needs with a nutritionist. Analysis of a sample of hair cut close to the scalp at the back of the head can provide an accurate record of minerals in the body and therefore helps determine deficiencies and excesses. Check with your doctor where analysis is available.
2 Always take vitamins immediately before or after food, never on an empty stomach.
3 Whenever possible, take vitamins packaged in a time-release formula which allows maximum absorption by releasing the vitamins slowly into the body.

Fruit and yoghurt energy shake

30 ml (2 tbsp) protein powder
30 ml (2 tbsp) lecithin powder
15 ml (1 tbsp) natural yeast
any fresh fruit
natural yoghurt
honey, to taste
3 ice cubes

Mix together and liquidize.

Milk and chocolate energy shake

30 ml (2 tbsp) protein powder
30 ml (2 tbsp) carob powder
milk
1 egg yolk
peanut butter, to taste

Mix together and liquidize.

Rosewater

4 parts fresh rose petals
1 part water

1 Gently simmer together for 15 minutes or until the fragrance is released.
2 Add the same amount of water and put in a bottle or atomizer.

Rich vitamin cream

100 ml (6½ tbsp) moisturising cream without synthetic oils or perfume
6 capsules synthetic vitamin A oil
6 capsules vitamin E oil

Break the capsules into the cream and stir until evenly blended.

Eye make-up remover pads

15 ml (1 tbsp) apricot kernel oil
15 ml (1 tbsp) water
cotton remover pads

Soak the remover pads in the oil and water and keep in a closed container.

Facial steam bath

camomile flowers or essence
2 capsules vitamin E oil
rosewater

1 Add the camomile flowers or essence to the water in a face steamer or large saucepan and infuse for 5-10 minutes.
2 Bring your face to the steam, closing your eyes, and sit for 10-15 minutes.
3 While the skin is warm and moist, massage the vitamin E oil directly into the skin.
4 Pat with rosewater.

lowest setting and move it around constantly. If you have long straight hair, stroke it with the palms of your hands, petting it in one direction like a cat's fur, to give it the same shine. This is how Jerry Hall, famous for her beautiful long hair, always keeps it so sleek and shiny. Only if it is dry should you follow the tradition of brushing it from the scalp for shine because this works by carrying oil from the sebaceous glands down to the tips of the hair.

Most hair that is out of condition is dry because it has lost its oils. Hair that has been permed, straightened or coloured is especially prone to that and needs constant conditioning. Follow the needs of your hair rather than orthodoxy: my hair is very dry and I find I need an extra-strength treatment cream intended for use once a month after every single wash because my hair sucks up conditioner like blotting paper. Dressing creams also help to bind together split ends and add shine; I carry around a tube of conditioner and dab it on when my hair feels like hay. Black women, who tend to have particularly dry, fragile hair, have used castor oil like this for centuries; an equally effective trick is to comb through a tiny bit of almond or jojoba oil. Iman sometimes also wets her hair, applies conditioner, lets it dry and wears it as a sleek pomade.

Though I dread the idle hours sitting around for a cut and professional treatment in John Frieda's salon, I always emerge with a fantastic head of hair, knowing that it was time well spent. It is that extra time and effort which turned the straw on my head into hair. To judge when it needs pruning, follow your own instinct: I always know by the dryness of the ends and Jerry Hall follows the waning of the moon because she swears it makes the hair grow faster. More prosaically, John recommends trimming off a centimetre every six weeks if you are trying to grow your hair.

How often you need a treatment depends on the conditon of your hair; without wholesale professional abuse, home treatments are probably enough. Many face foods can also be used for the hair: I use mayonnaise, my special body cream and avocado, for example, and John Frieda recommends olive or almond oil. Another easy enrichment is an egg yolk added to your normal conditioner.

Whatever the treatment, rub it into the ends of the hair, or massage it into the scalp as well, then cover with a cap or towel and leave it for as long as you can. If I am lying in the sun, I often apply conditioner, tie my hair in a knot and leave it like that for hours. Heat also makes any treatment more effective by opening up the hair shafts and allowing the oils to penetrate more quickly: this may be done with a hot towel or in a sauna, or by applying warm oil directly to the scalp. Always shampoo well at the end so your hair does not smell like a deli counter.

Once in a while, usually on a Sunday, I like to give myself a more complete therapy session. First, I check that I am completely clean and cared for from head to toe. I start by filing my nails, cleaning my face with rosewater and taking one of my quick, steamy baths. Next, I feed all my body surfaces, massaging in rich body cream into the ends of my hair, my face and the rough patches of my body. Then I tie my hair back into a knot and dunk my feet into a basin of warm water and olive oil for several minutes. Afterwards I wash my face and use a moisturizing face mask. Finally I wash my hair and shave my legs, or perhaps give myself a bikini wax. By the time I emerge from the bathroom I feel completely refreshed and revived.

But that is only a small part of my day of rest. Then I forget the surface and devote the rest of the day to the parts which really matter: the mind and spirit. I have met many women and men considered to be beauties, but so often it stops there. A surfeit of surface beauty makes one long for something more. Without the glow of a warm spirit a body is hollow; without compassionate beliefs eyes lack real sparkle and faces are empty masks with a painted expression of glitter or gloss. Physical energy is also only part of the story – a superficial form of health unless it is balanced by the capacity to give back what you take. That ability is founded on inner strength and peace and that is why I call body philosophy internal style.

Body skin needs just as much care and nourishment as your face, even if it does spend a lot of the year buried under clothes.

STYLE

tyle is a question of remaining true to yourself and never being bought off from your own values and memories. It hinges on originality and conviction, being able to laugh with others, and at yourself, through your taste and life style. In the eighties, it has become something quite different – a designer label to be displayed and sold, a narcissistic obsession defined by other people. To me, that misses the point completely. Style is, after all, a guideline through the bewildering barrage of a consumer culture, a personal language expressing individual choice and personality. But if you are more concerned with your own image than the imagery around you and you start to follow other people's instructions instead of your judgments then you will simply get lost. I do not think of style as something which belongs only to fashion – or even clothes as its most important expression – but I do find it easiest to work out what style is in fashion terms because that is my business. Yves St Laurent once said that he often draws inspiration from his models because they evolve their own style by abandoning fashions to wear what suits them. I think that is the heart of the matter: models know professionally that if you do not feel comfortable with the clothes you are showing, you lose confidence and, with that, the whole effect. The same holds true away from the catwalk. Clothes are the most personal and easily controlled way of showing the rest of the world how you see yourself, and of making sure that other people see you in that way. That is why caring about the way you look is much more than vanity.

The message of clothes is in part unintentional, through the element of shared taste which grows out of culture and climate, time and place. Look at the way female fashion reflects the shifts in economy and political mood: the extravagance of Dior's post-war New Look, the explosion of young affluence and self-confidence in the extreme clothes of the youthful sixties, the fragmented, searching post-feminist seventies and, finally, today's fickle, eclectic outbursts as the eighties gather speed. Contemporary national design style says a lot too: American sporty leisurewear, continental tailored chic and elegance, English non-conformist street-fashion. Japanese style is a particularly interesting case because after decades of immaculate dressing following Western taste, the Japanese designers have developed a distinctive style abandoning the European aesthetics of cut and line for sizeless shapes built around the drape, texture and weave of the fabric.

The emergence of a new style or look cannot be created at will, although a particular photographer or designer may be highly influential, because it is always a question of mood and international market response. I have often been described as the model epitomising the hard-edged, sleek

Two of the most stylish women I know – Tina Chow (left) and Loulou de la Falaise (right). I love Tina's knack for combining simplicity and extravagance – in this case a band-aid T-shirt with twenties Chanel jewellery. Loulou has a much more aggressive look, both outrageous and sexy.

sophistication of the seventies. In fashion terms, that mood expressed itself as an aggressive chic exploring artificial colours, synthetic fibres and a sense of the dramatic; in modelling as the rediscovery of sultry passion and the exotic woman, who had already flashed by in the twenties and whose prototype this time was Bianca Jagger; in photography as the cynical, sometimes almost threatening work of Helmut Newton. It first showed itself in England early in the decade, was quickly taken up in America and much later found its way to Paris in the work of the young stars of the late seventies, Claude Montana and Thierry Mugler, who took it to a sinister, sexually ambivalent extreme.

But style is also highly personal and a great deal more international than that. Some people seem to be born with the certainty and self-confidence needed to explore their own taste and go their own way from the start. In this sense, I am sure style can be inherited. Certainly that is true within fashion: to take just two examples, look at Paloma Picasso, whose style is so reminiscent of her father's spirit – unashamedly sexy, sometimes deliberately outrageous and very Latin – and Angelica Huston, whose bold anti-classical severity captures the glamorous charisma of the film world. Then there are those who inherit a hybrid style: Tina Chow, whose Japanese-American eye combines extravagance and simplicity, antique and modern, with a gloriously uncluttered freedom; Loulou de la Falaise, who throws together brash colours and sophisticated cut in a unique American-French *mélange*.

But memory is not only inherited. Look at Coco Chanel, who drew so explicitly on her past: her smock tops echoed those of French school children and her love of everything English, from pearls and tweeds to

cardigans and suits, sprang from her passionate love for Boy Capel, a polo-playing Englishman who was killed in a car crash only four years after they met. Chanel detailed all her clothes with such memories. But most of all she cared about design to suit the modern woman. Her starting point was, rightly, life style – to make clothes that women could 'live in, feel comfortable in and breathe in'. That was the key to her style, which made her comeback in the fifties at the age of eighty such a phenomenal success. By then, elaborate Paris glamour had once again forgotten comfort and the beauty of the natural female form – a simple mistake, but one that it took a woman to spot. It is that eye for form and lifestyle which should provide the key momentum for change, in shared as well as individual taste. Clothes which make men and women slaves to a particular look may be fashion and they may sell, but they are not style. They are stylized.

My own tastes are partly inherited and partly those of a child of the islands – a balance of natural beauty and glamour, a meeting of East and West. The Japanese side of me has always loved flowers and perfumes, balanced elegance and quality, with a pinch of mystery and magic thrown in. That is the teasing, flirting side of my nature; the American side of me wants independence and adventure, sophistication and glamour, but in an unorthodox way. Temperamentally, that is the side of me which stubbornly goes its own way. Both sides likes to laugh. The roots of that style were laid down by the end of my childhood, but I did not become conscious of it until much later in life.

That is simply a measure of how long it took me to find my self-confidence. In my pre-teens, I simply wanted to look like everyone else. I could see that the glamour of Gina Lollobrigida, Ava Gardner and the Sunmaid girl was more than physical beauty, but all I could do was try and imitate their trademarks which I believed would transform me from an ugly duckling into a swan. That was not very easy given that my idealized woman had curls and curves and that my own trademarks were frizzy hair and skinny ribs. Even my parents could see the problem. They tried to help by buying me contact lenses so I could get rid of my glasses, but all I really wanted were the curves and curls.

How could I find the curves? I found a good remedy for my straight hips – padding them out with layers of knickers. My resolutely flat chest was more difficult. I eventually spotted the solution in Liberty House, the biggest downtown store: a five-dollar bra which came to life, like waterwings, when you blew through a little straw. Unfortunately, my car washing money would not stretch to five dollars, so I adapted the idea to the expandable bra Mom had optimistically bought me and stuffed it with tissue paper. Then one day I was humiliatingly discovered when I used yellow paper under a white T-shirt and I had to abandon my fake curves for fear of mockery. This taught me the importance of simple colour schemes.

My consolation lay in my salty, sun-bleached frizz of hair, which provided me with a curtain to hide behind. Then came the unfortunate scalping by Vidal Sassoon. Lured by an advertisement offering $100 to any girl with exceptionally long hair, I offered myself up as a model at a hairdressing demonstration he was doing at a Honolulu hotel. After he had been at work with his razor and a tiny pair of scissors for about half an hour, my neck felt suspiciously bare and cold. Everyone burst into wild applause. I knew from Mom's expression, however, that all was not well, and when I finally found a mirror I came face to face with a geometrically lopped giraffe. With my small-town Honolulu tastes all I wanted was sexy, long

A shot taken during the French collections for British *Vogue*. We started the shoot around 9 p.m. This was one of the last pictures we did – around 5 a.m. I was so exhausted by this time, I could hardly hold the pose. As it was, *Vogue* never published the picture.

hair like every other surfer girl and I was so horrified at the idea of what my friends would think that I cut class for a week. I still get a failure of nerves every time I contemplate a brave new cut.

At a certain stage, I woke up to the fact that I could never look like my screen heroines. Then, however, as my daring unorthodox spirit came to the fore, I came upon the notion of unconventional beauty. This was also the time that I discovered my visualization techniques: the book said I had to be positive, think radiant. The result was the weird look, wearing huge sunglasses and ironing my hair flat, whitening my face with baby powder and going off to rock concerts draped in a purple toga lovingly run up by Suzon with matching bougainvillea in my hair. That was my first discovery of The Total Look. Very positive. By the time of be-ins and love-ins I was doing a daring routine which I called interpretative dancing, and painting myself silver. Very radiant.

It was shortly after this that I became Kanebo's cute, leggy little beauty and, suddenly transplanted from my native soil, lapsed into uncharacteristic timidity and silence. Once I had found my feet, I settled down in Tokyo, but when I arrived in London I felt swamped all over again, this time by my delicate oriental image. Suzon was horrified when she once came on a session with me so I had to explain to her that London fashion was just discovering the rest of the world, and that I did not think they were ready yet for the real Hawaiian girl. As my image became a sort of universal exoticism – anything from Latin American to Indian, Tahitian, Chinese, Mexican and Eskimo – I began increasingly to dislike this impersonal, sexless creature. To my eyes she was not charmingly mysterious, but a stereotype who was not allowed sophistication, wit or warmth.

Through Bailey, I began to find the balance again and transcended what everyone else wanted to see in me for my own personality and interpretation of elegance and glamour. For the camera my parts became more varied – we did everything from *Shanghai Express* to *Death in Venice*, a strip poker sequence to the *Arabian Nights* – but I followed my own way of interpreting them and began to feel ill-at-ease with any images which clashed with that. I found myself posing differently and even looking at the camera in an unfamiliar, ill-at-ease way if I had to wear something silly like a short blonde wig. Then I began to experience the same feelings on the catwalk: if I had to have my hair scraped back into a tight chignon, or turn on tricksy effects, like a mock strip routine with zips and scarves, I felt like bolting back to the dressing room. My own walk developed as a slightly flirty, but understated style which swung but never broke into a dance, a sexiness which was for women as much as men.

Away from the camera and the catwalk I also began to feel a much stronger sense of my style. In Japan, I had breathed a sigh of relief at escaping gaudy tropical colours and begun to dress in black for winter and white for summer, which married well with the uncluttered neatness of Japanese style. Beyond that I simply wore exactly what I wanted, but always resisted anything that looked too perfect; I hated the idea that I might become a fashion victim almost without realizing it. The essence of my off-balance style was there, but I did not have the confidence to wear it that way. Bailey gave me that missing ingredient. I remember arriving for work one morning in the very early days dressed in baggy trousers, an old trench coat and a squashed fedora hat, which were literally the first things I had pulled out of the cupboard that morning. When Bailey said how good it looked and what a great sense of style I had, I was astonished.

Contrasting styles: fifties glamour (left) and the casual look (above) in which I'm wearing one of my favourite jackets – I've had it since I was fifteen years old.

But as the years went by I realized that I did have quite firm ideas about what I felt good in. Sometimes in Paris Bailey would offer to buy me some wonderfully stylish outfit, but I would always refuse if it felt too strict and perfectly coordinated for my own quirky independence. I hate wearing other people's fashion statements which swamp my own character. Gradually I began to enjoy my old fantasies too. First, back came the curls I had dreamed of since my trips to the drive-in. Then came the curves. Around this time I began to give myself a waist by clinching in anything loose with a belt. Finally, the aura arrived. After years of trying duty-free perfumes which came out on me smelling like cheap bubble gum, I found a musky tea-rose scent with no air of imitation about it which clung to me in just the right way. As I used to spray it on I would hear Bailey down in the studio, complaining about the stink of the rosewater wafting around the house, but it never stopped me. It has become almost a part of me, and certainly something of my mystery. Now I would not give away its origin any more than I would the closest secrets of my private life.

As I began to play around more consciously with my taste and memories, I evolved an easy stylishness which suited both my temperament and my life style: a blend of muted Eastern sophistication and jokey American glamour. But the most important thing was that they took my unpredictable day as their starting point. I needed clothes to put on and then forget for the rest of the day, for running or the Ritz, to take me from washing up after breakfast through a business lunch and then back home again for an evening curled up in a chair watching television.

Taken as a package deal, there was not a designer or look which left me comfortable, glamorous and free to go anywhere in my own style, so I devised my own look, putting together a little of everything, but leaving plenty of room on the top for my own fun and a few fantasies. It is a look which borrows a lot – the million-dollar glamour of the continentals and the casual feel of American leisurewear, the elegance and fine fabrics of the Japanese and the humour of the English – but in each case discards the complete statement – the sleek stiffness, the down-to-earth sportiness, and the strength of line and cut which I find swamping.

I designed that look in the mirror at home, and when I could not find the basics I needed, I made them with the help of friends who let me choose my own fabrics. Of course, I was lucky, because I knew the best designers – the Emanuels, Bruce Oldfield and Anthony Price – but I do think that any woman can achieve the same effect with the help of a sewing machine or an inexpensive seamstress. After all, my starting point was Suzon's purple toga. I still use lots of homemade tricks: if jumpers and T-shirts are not as loose as I like them, then I simply stretch them to the right size, and I am often taking out shoulder pads, or even cutting and re-sewing a neckline.

For me, as for most people, style has to be good value. I invest in a small wardrobe of interchangeable basics for summer and winter, which can be varied endless ways with different make-up and accessories. For the day that means well-cut trousers, skirts, and several shirts and sweaters. Since I am far more fickle with my evening clothes, I keep all my old ones in an enormous trunk and two or three times a year rediscover old gems. Another trick from the days of *haute-couture* is to have favourites copied. From the ready-to-wear mentality, remember that it is economical rather than extravagant to buy two of anything that you know you will wear until it is falling apart at the seams. Old-fashioned or specialist stores are far more likely to give you value combined with quality than fashion shops and smart

This photograph was originally taken as a landscape. But Bailey so liked the print upright that we have used it that way ever since.

CASUAL GLAMOUR

Evening is the time to enjoy your fantasies. I find it all becomes too serious if I feel overdressed, so I always look for casual glamour, the sophistication comes from the elegant simplicity of black and white, with costume jewellery against luxurious velvet, *crêpe de chine*, raw silk and cashmere; the casual look comes from putting basic pieces together in off-beat combinations.

A cashmere T-shirt dress
A taffeta full skirt
A white silk blouse
A bustier, or strapless swimsuit
A man's baggy jacket
A pair of evening trousers
A sexy sweater
A straight skirt
A sequined cardigan

1 Gypsy style: a full skirt, which comes to just above the ankles, and a plain T-shirt stretched to fit off the shoulders, with a splash of red taffeta and a red flower at the waist and gold charms and hoop earrings.

2 Hollywood glamour: a straight black skirt worn with the bustier or strapless swimsuit, jazzed up by a diamanté belt, lots of sparkly costume jewellery, very inexpensive evening gloves and a simple length of net.

3 Cocktail chic: the straight skirt teamed with a black sweater, falling casually off one shoulder, with crystal jewellery, fishnet stockings and bright red shoes.

4 Full dress: the evening trousers and white shirt with a man's dinner jacket on top. So that it will not look too severe, I have pinned up my hair, but carried the look through to the jewellery.

5 Designer chic: the cashmere sweater dress worn with the sequined cardigan and jewellery that will not outdazzle the cardigan.

6 Sophisticated leisurewear: black evening trousers teamed with a white silk blouse, knotted at the waist, and a sequined cardigan slung over the shoulders. I have added a belt and fake pearl earrings, necklace and bracelets.

Key to photographs on following pages

labels; shirts and sweaters, for instance, are much better buys at men's shops. Accessories should also talk effect rather than bank balance; splashy fake jewels can be just as stylish as real sparklers and are far less worry.

Style must also be comfortable and versatile. The uninhibited freedom of light tropical clothes has left me with a permanent dislike of heavy and cramping clothes. I like plenty of space for easy movement – stretchy or baggy trousers, roomy shirts and jumpers and well-fitting cotton tops; I hate tight jeans, skirts a size too small which feel like a corset or crippling high heels, which turn walking into an agonizing hobble. I also hate hours of planning but want lots of room for last-minute improvisation.

The way I manage to combine all this is by sticking to my plain black and white backdrops, which take me anywhere from a hot summer's day to a smart winter's evening, but leave plenty of scope to go to town with the finishing touches – not perfectly co-ordinated accessories, but tongue-in-cheek details which throw everything slightly off-key by throwing in a little daring or a touch of witty glamour, depending on my feelings on the day. As with everything, it comes down not only to what you do, but also the way that you do it – not so much the clothes you are wearing, but the way you put them together. I particularly love over-accessorizing classic clothes with flashy jewellery, brightly coloured scarves, shawls and belts, splashy red fingernails, or fun props like a pair of fishnet tights or a shawl made out of an old piece of black net.

The total look only ever comes together in the mirror, not as studied perfection but by playing off two moods against each other. My favourites are men's clothes turned on their head to look feminine, or a clash between the sober and the frivolous, the demure and the sexy. The wit and conviction have to be carried down to the right details. The most important rule with stolen men's clothes is to wear them as they were designed to be worn. That was why Marlene Dietrich looked so marvellous in a man's trousers and shirt – it was the shoes, the sleek hair, the tie and the beret which looked so good. Ava Gardner gave the same kind of style a jazzy fifties touch, dressing up men's clothes with lots of fun jewellery and tight belts, keeping her hair high on her head.

I try to think through that kind of detail in the same way. Jeans go with sneakers and cowboy boots, as they were meant to be worn in Wyoming or Texas; baggy men's trousers and jackets look great in the city with brogues or Minnie Mouse pumps, depending on how boyish or feminine you want to look. Which way you swing the detail depends on the length of your hair. If I am wearing a man's suit in the evening, then I pile my hair on top of my head and keep the accessories down to a bare minimum, but during the day, when I always have my hair down, I keep in some deliberately feminine details like dangly earrings, or a brightly coloured scarf.

If you are playing off the demure against the sexy, the sober against the frivolous, the basic rule is restraint with the background. During the day, I will wear a very plain knee-length pencil skirt with a roomy man's sweater or shirt, but then leave a glimpse of a lacy vest or slip the top off one shoulder, and perhaps add fishnet or patterned tights. In the evening, I keep the backdrop even more severe, with plain black clothes covering me from neck to ankle and down to the wrists – and then dress up with casually worn jewellery, piling on strings of fake pearls, crystal or diamanté necklaces and gold chains – around neck, wrists and waist. If the emphasis during the day is on comfort, in the evening it is on glamour.

Now that I have evolved that casual glamour I would never abandon it,

Casual glamour for the day by Issey Miyake. This fashion shot, unlike many others, actually reflects how I like to look outside work.

whatever fashion may bring. Of course, I am sure that my style will go on evolving and no doubt the personal quirks will change, but now I know myself, I also know exactly how I want to be seen. People say it is lucky to be born of two bloods, to have something of two worlds in yourself and it is true in some ways. But it can also make it more difficult to discover exactly who you are. It was never a problem for me when I was growing up in Hawaii, but when I went to Japan and then came to Europe, I found it hard because I did not feel at ease with the delicate little oriental girl people perceived me to be and I felt like squashing her completely with the headstrong hoyden.

It was through the loss of Suzon's gentle spirit that I finally discovered myself. I realised that if style sprang from memories and conviction, the ability to laugh with others and at myself, then it was something to spread right through my life, just as Suzon had done in hers. Style may be harder to pin down in this less clearly defined meaning, but it is still easy to recognize. It was my father giving me a plane ticket to Tokyo instead of a gold watch, and the way my uncle devotedly stroked his goldfish. It was Billy's kiss and Bailey's shoes. It spreads laughter and the love of life wherever it goes because it knows how to take and how to give back with meaning: it is the passionate friendship Bailey has always shown me. It cherishes the things which really matter – natural beauty, the quality of life and the affection of good friends – and it has the generosity of spirit to express that in the smallest details.

There is one thing of which I am sure above all else. Style means knowing yourself.

Photographic Acknowledgements

The author and publishers wish to thank the following photographers by whose kind permission the illustrations are reproduced: Michel Arnaud: 82; Clive Arrowsmith: 26, 27, 158; David Bailey: frontispiece, 9, 14, 22, 28, 32, 33, 39, 45, 50, 51, 55, 56, 57, 59, 66, 70, 71, 75, 77, 80, 86, 88, 91, 92, 93, 95, 96, 98, 100, 101, 103, 106, 107, 108, 109, 113, 115, 116, 119, 120, 122, 128, 130, 131, 132, 134, 137, 138, 139, 144, 145, 146, 147, 149, 151, 152, 157, 160, 161, 162, 164, 165, 167, 168, 173, 176; Gianpaulo Barbieri: 35; Tony Boase: 174; Alan Davidson: 52; Hiroshi: 25; François Lamy: 90; Jacques Henri Lartigue: 43, 79; Barry Lategan: 30, 31; Patrick Lichfield: 73; David Montgomery: 82, 83; Helmut Newton: 40, 41, 42, 58, 72; Shinoyama: 19; Alice Springs: 46, 161; John Swannell: 63, Tony Viramontes (illustrator): 124; Richard Young: 60, 74.

Thanks are also due to the following publications, institutions and individuals who released or loaned photographs: Martine d'Astier and Isabelle Jammes: Association des Amis de Jacques Henri Lartigue: 43, 79; courtesy of Company/National Magazine Co Ltd: 158; courtesy of Harpers and Queen/National Magazine Co Ltd: 25, 131, 138; Mr Ishizaka and Kanebo Cosmetics, Tokyo: 19; Olympus Cameras: 32, 33; Ritz Newspapers: 40, 93, 113, 173; Yves St Laurent: 88, 96; Times Newspapers: 69; Gianni Versace: 34; by courtesy of British Vogue, © Condé Nast Publications Ltd: frontispiece, 15, 26, 27, 30, 31, 50, 51, 55, 56, 57, 66, 86, 98, 103, 132, 139, 146, 147, 148, 149, 160, 162, 168; by courtesy of French Vogue, © Condé Nast Publications Ltd, 59, 107, 151; by courtesy of Italian Vogue © Condé Nast Publications Ltd: 66, 70, 71, 90, 91, 95, 100, 101, 103, 115, 122, 130, 134; courtesy of Woman magazine: 174.

Thanks also to: Yves St Laurent, Chanel, Benny Ong, Whistles, Gianni Versace, Browns, Butler and Wilson: 168, 169.